THE ANGRY CHILD

Sleeping Giant or Paper Tiger?

by

Kim J. Masters, M.D.

Other Books Available

DEDICATION

To GERALDINE

ACKNOWLEDGEMENTS

I would like to thank Margaret McCaffrey for the creative editorial support and for her contributions of the material about divorce and *The Hurried Child*; Janet Chilnick of the PIA Press for the editorial support in the transformation of turgid prose to conversational narrative; Judy Warren for her comments, extensive secretarial support, and her encouragement; Tesla Hood for her administrative support; Joe Masters for the lesson that preaching is easier than listening; Shady Masters, for her views, support, and knowledge, an Walter Masters, for his many contributions to my knowledge about concern and caring.

CONTENTS

PREFACE

Anger is a powerful response that we continually encounter in ourselves and others. It is a frightening emotion, one that many of us do not understand. It manifests itself in countless behaviors, and many of us feel ill-equipped to cope with its expression.

In this book, Dr. Kim Masters does a brilliant job of helping us understand the complicated emotion of anger. He explains it as it relates to: our emotional selves, our physical selves, our families, and the external factors that may contribute to its expression in children and adolescents. Dr. Masters also provides some useful and practical tools for helping parents manage their children. He explains how anger can be used constructively to improve the parent-child relationship.

As evidenced in this book, the author has touched the lives of many children, and he has seen anger in many forms. As Administrator of Appalachian Hall, I have the utmost in respect and admiration for Dr. Kim Masters. I have talked personally with many of the children and adolescents who are under his care. It is Dr. Masters' commitment to his profession and his commitment to the lives and families of the children he treats that makes this a useful book for all of us to read.

Jay Cutspec
Administrator, Appalachian Hall

KIM J. MASTERS, M.D.

Kim J. Masters, M.D. is Medical Director of the Adolescent and Children's Programs at Appalachian Hall in Asheville, North Carolina. He received his doctorate in medicine from Harvard Medical School. Dr. Masters is Board Certified in Child and Adolescent Psychiatry, and is nationally known for his expertise in working with troubled children and adolescents. He is also a Fellow of the American Academy of Child Psychiatry and a Fellow of the American College of Physicians.

INTRODUCTION: VOLCANO OR HOUSE OF CARDS?

Like a sleeping, brooding giant, anger resides in all of us, resting quietly until something occurs to arouse it and unleash its fearsome power.

Whether it's an unkind word or a frustrating event which awakens the anger in us, the results are very similar. When we perceive something as threatening, our brains react with a series of electrochemical discharges that send alarm signals throughout the body. Outwardly, this might result in a hostile glance, a pointing finger, a raised voice, or a cutting remark. Inwardly, our hearts start beating faster and our adrenaline begins to surge. As a result, our muscles tense, our blood vessels constrict, and our stomachs tighten up. The accompanying feelings might be ones of resentment, exasperation, annoyance, irritation, indignation, or, in its extreme, intense rage and fury.

After our flash of anger is spent, we are often embarrassed, ashamed, and in trouble. We see that what may have seemed like power is actually impotence. What made us momentarily feel like a fearsome giant, in the long run shows us to be vulnerable and weak.

ANGER: A NORMAL PART OF LIFE

Anger is a normal, pervasive emotion. But it's one about which there is much misunderstanding. Expressed and handled correctly, anger promotes understanding and cooperation between family members and peers. If someone we are close to is annoying us or doing things that we think are unfair, telling them is the first step toward negotiating an improvement in the relationship.

But many of us feel that we shouldn't be angry with our friends and families, so we keep it inside and let it build up. Unfortunately, this can have more negative consequences than the constructive expression of anger; it leads to sarcasm, emotional distancing, and misunderstanding. Bottled-up anger may exacerbate physical illnesses and can be a factor in psychological disorders, such as depression. Being able to accept and express normal feelings of anger in a constructive and nonaggressive way promotes emotional health and satisfying relationships with others.

WHEN ANGER GETS OUT OF CONTROL

On the other hand, poorly controlled or misplaced anger can do enormous damage. Showing anger in attacking or destructive ways usually inflames disagreements between family members and rarely leads to a resolution of differences. If anger becomes the predominant way that individuals communicate with each other, it creates even more anger with no resolution.

It can become a way of life!

Angry individuals are often brittle, although they may appear strong. They often find it difficult to cope with stress in any way other than becoming hostile.

Or parents and children might use anger as a means of coercion to get what they want from each other. When anger is used in these negative ways, it often engenders deep resentment. Chronic anger in family communications can undermine discipline and impede emotional growth.

If children grow up without ever getting a handle on their tempers, they are likely to go through life having difficulties with others. If they don't learn to control their anger, their anger will control them, almost always with negative consequences.

THE ANGRY CHILD

"I don't want to go. You can't make me go. I hate you!" That's Joshua screaming at his mother. He's just jumped up and down by the kitchen door. He's just kicked the pile of newspapers for recycling.

"Why do you do this to me!" This comment stops Joshua's mother cold. She'd been walking over to him, ready to take his arm and pull him over to a chair, where, finger pointing, she'd yell at him to stay quiet until she said he could get up.

But this last remark puzzled her. It made her confused, guilty. What was she doing to her child—and what was he doing to her?

Joshua's mother was becoming a victim, not of her child but of anger. Joshua was angry, plain and simple, and, instead of just punishing its distressing overt signs, she should be examining what's going on inside him.

Then, and only then, can the anger disappear.

It is my purpose in this book to help those of you, like Joshua's mother, who find anger a disruptive element in your family. It is drawn from many years of working with children and adolescents whose anger has alienated them from other family members and has gotten them into trouble with their peers, at school, or on a job. It is also based on my experience with those young people who have been victimized by being unable to stand up to or cope with the anger they experience from others—especially from peers. And it comes from my work with individuals who have been physically or sexually abused, from helping them deal with the justified anger they feel without it taking over their lives in destructive ways.

It is my hope to increase your understanding of anger— its signs, sources, and biological underpinnings—and to give you specific strategies to help you deal with it effectively in your children. These strategies should enable you to help your children or adolescents take responsibility for their anger, to learn to control it themselves, and, ultimately, to be able to express anger in nonaggressive yet effective ways.

Understanding anger may improve your parenting skills. This insight, along with the individual techniques I suggest, should give you the ability to step out of the role of doormat or ineffective disciplinarian.

Hopefully, this, in turn, will bring greater strength to your family and its individual members.

CHAPTER ONE

ANGER'S MANY EXPRESSIONS AND SOURCES

Consider the following:

- "Screaming Laura," age 7, lives with her sister, Emily, age 14, and her mother and father. Emily gets upset easily and often screams and yells at Laura, pulls her hair, and tells her to get out of the way. When Laura's parents go to a teacher's conference, they are told that Laura has been picking on younger children in class, screaming and yelling at them, pulling their hair, and calling them names.

When children experience anger from others, they may practice it themselves. Some other examples of the different expressions of anger children may learn from family members:

- "Yelling 10-Year-Old Harry" frequently hears his brother, Robert, 17, screaming and yelling at his parents when he doesn't get his way.

---

*Patient names, and their identifying characteristics, have been changed to protect privacy.

- "Crying Rebecca," age 5, silently watches her mother, Alice, cry in frustration when things go wrong at home.
- "Silent Ward," 6 years old, sees his sister, Lavenina, 15, hang up the phone on her boyfriend and refuse to talk to him after an argument. He notices the same thing happen between his sister and his family when she disagrees with them.
- "Self-Abuse Valerie," age 7, sees her 15-year-old sister, Ann, bang her head on the table when she feels that she had made a stupid mistake.
- "Leave in the Middle Anthony," age 9, watches his dad leave home and go for a walk when he is angry—instead of continuing an argument in the kitchen.

Though the underlying physiological mechanisms of anger are similar in these and all other cases, its expressions and sources are varied and complex. The following "Sore Subjects" should give you a better understanding of what may lie behind the anger you see in your children and adolescents.

SORE SUBJECT # 1: Anger Learned by Modeling

Day-to-day life in a family is the most effective school for learning how to act. In the ongoing psychodrama of family life, interactions between parents, between parents and children, and between children themselves, serve as models that children unconsciously imitate and incorporate into their own repertoire of behaviors. Unless they make a conscious decision to do otherwise, or undergo therapy or behavioral treatment of some kind, people will probably draw on their childhood experience throughout life, repeating the same patterns in their relationships as they experienced with their parents. Chances are they will do to their children what their parents did to them.

The ways in which you and your children express anger are very likely to be mirrored in each other's behavior.

SORE SUBJECT # 2: Family Disruption— Divorce and Discord

Much of what I will say in later chapters is based on the assumption that your family is a pretty healthy one, free of serious marital discord. However, since at least half of first marriages and an estimated two-thirds of second marriages now end in divorce, I want to address how this kind of disruption might be the source of your child's anger.

When marriages start to break down, there is usually a great deal of tension and discord between the parents. If there isn't out-and-out open warfare, there might be sniping, sarcasm, or emotional distancing between spouses, which is as hurtful as screaming and arguing. In either case, the negative emotions and uncertainty that fill the atmosphere when a marriage is faltering inevitably affect children. Since most children can't express their feelings directly about something so painful as their parents' potential or actual divorce, they usually act out those feelings.

And the most common emotion children use in "acting out" during divorce is anger.

Thus, if your marriage is in trouble, your children's angry behavior could very well be a reflection of family tensions. It's important for you to realize this in order for you to get the proper help. Though the strategies that I will be offering should be useful, you might also need marital or family counseling to ease the tensions in your home and to help your child work through the anger at its source.

Divorce alone is not the sole culprit. If battling has become the way you and your spouse tend to communicate, this, too, will probably be reflected in your children's behavior. Many people are unaware of how frequently they argue or of the undercurrents of anger and tension that exist in their marital relationship. Perhaps this was the way their parents behaved, so they do it unconsciously themselves.

Emotions and actions at home almost always resonate in children. Even if divorce is not a question, but you have

---

"SEEING RED"
Some Ways People Show Anger

Yelling	Spending money
Hitting	Using drugs and/or alcohol
Destroying things	Withdrawing
Crying	Laughing
Being silent	Discounting
Complaining	Interrupting
Getting someone else to be angry	Ruminating and worrying
Getting someone else to show revenge	Acting in self-destructive and self-abusive ways
Walking out	Refusing to go to school

---

fallen into the habit of chronic warfare, you should seek family counseling if you want your child's problem behavior to improve.

SORE SUBJECT # 3: Family Dysfunction—Mental or Physical Illness in the Family

In recent years, psychologists and psychiatrists have been intensely studying families to try to understand the many forces that operate within them. As a result, families have come to be viewed as systems, much like the human body itself, with interdependent parts, each with its own function. Ideally, all members play their parts, and the family functions smoothly.

But there are any number of things that can go wrong and render the family dysfunctional. As I noted above, divorce or marital discord can cause family dysfunction. One family member having a serious mental or physical illness can also throw the family system out of kilter. In these cases, other members often have to overcompensate to keep the family afloat.

For example, if one parent is alcoholic or seriously depressed, the other might have to work harder to keep finances in line or to take care of the children. The children themselves might assume different roles to make up for the failing parent. One child might take on the hero role, becoming a superachiever to offset the family's other failures. Or one child might become the "bad" one or scapegoat, unconsciously acting out and becoming a symbol for all that is wrong in the family. These scapegoated children are particularly relevant to our discussion because they often exhibit a lot of angry behavior that parents tend to misinterpret.

If any of your family members are suffering from chemical dependence, depression, or other psychiatric or serious physical disorders that might be causing dysfunction, I strongly suggest that you seek family counseling. As illustrated above, these kinds of problems cause an enormous amount of tension that, more times than not, resonate in children.

When illness becomes chronic, it's a mistake to assume that you have a problem child if he or she is misbehaving or disagreeable. The fact is that your son or daughter might be reacting to the problems in your family. It's important to recognize this and to get the proper help early—which can, perhaps, avoid more serious problems as the child gets older.

SORE SUBJECT # 4: Hurried Children

In his groundbreaking book *The Hurried Child*, psychologist David Elkind admonished us about the many ways children are being forced to grow up too soon in our society today. We pressure them in the schools, encourage them to wear adult-looking clothes, and rush them through their childhoods with nonstop activities. This kind of hurrying creates a lot of stress for children and can lead to a wide variety of psychological problems. Angry and aggressive behavior is one of the many symptoms a child might exhibit when he or she feels too pushed and too pressured. Although it's a potent force, we're all so caught up in this "hurrying" process that it's easy for parents to overlook it as a factor in their child's misbehavior.

SORE SUBJECT # 5: Difficult Temperaments

Children born with what have come to be known as "difficult" temperaments tend to have trouble controlling anger. These "difficult" youngsters were first recognized by Stella Chess and Thomas Chess in a landmark research project which found that as many as 15 percent of all children exhibit certain personality traits that make them difficult to raise. As early as three months of age, these children show a tendency to:

- Be irritable
- Sleep irregularly
- Eat in a fussy manner
- Be overly sensitive to touch
- Have frequent bad moods
- Get upset in new situations
- Withdraw from relatives and strangers
- Be very intense

Getting angry may be another key feature of their personalities.

But many children who fall into this "difficult" category are not easy to spot. Because they are often not properly diagnosed, these children can get labeled as "bad" or disagreeable by parents and teachers; they can grow up with damaged self-esteem. As a result, they often end up with serious behavior disorders that could have been buffered if proper treatment had been obtained.

If your child exhibits any of the above traits of a "difficult" temperament, you should have him evaluated. I also recommend reading *The Difficult Child* by Dr. Stanley Turecki, which describes this syndrome and offers many helpful strategies.

SORE SUBJECT # 6: Underlying Psychiatric Disorders

Anger in children or adolescents could be the result of an underlying psychiatric disorder, such as depression, an oppositional behavior disorder, brain damage, or epilepsy. These are so important that I've devoted more space to them in the next chapter.

SORE SUBJECT # 7: Situations Are Important, Too

As we have seen, children's anger and the way they express it can arise from any number of different sources within the family and within themselves. But in order to fully understand what's going on when your child explodes at any given time, you need to identify what it was in that situation that triggered an angry response. It could be something as serious as experiencing an abusive trauma at home or at school—or as minor as a fight with a friend. In later chapters, I will help sensitize you to some of the elements in your children's lives that might be contributing to their anger.

My goal in this chapter, and throughout this book, is to demonstrate the complexity of children's anger. I believe that's the first step toward helping them to control it. Let's delve deeper.

CHAPTER TWO

DOES ANGER HAVE A VOLUME CONTROL?

Most of us tend to think of anger almost as though it were a natural force, like a volcano or a tornado. Once it erupts—once it snatches us into its whirlwind—we assume that it cannot be slowed down or easily quieted. But is that really true?

Let's look at the example of 15-year-old Hilda, whose mother has told her that she cannot go out Saturday night. Hilda immediately raises her voice. She yells and screams. She throws her shoe at her mother, stomps off, and slams the door, shouting, "I hate you!" as she storms off to her room. Her mother then turns to her father and says, "Well, Hilda's bad temper is flaring up again."

Though many parents would not react with such equanimity to such a scene, in this case, the mother assumes that her daughter's anger is her way of coping with disappointment. Even though she is upset, she is resigned to her daughter's bad temper, and she feels that there is no way she can change it. But let's replay the scene with a provocative twist.

This time, we will let the action proceed as before, until the point where Hilda picks up her shoe with the intention of throwing it. Now, instead of just standing there, her mother takes a $20 bill from her wallet and says, "If you can cut out this behavior and act civilly for half an hour, I'll give you this twenty-dollar bill."

What do you think Hilda would say? Would she say, "No, I can't control myself" or, "Sure, give me the twenty dollars." In my experience, the latter is the more likely response. And the reason for this is quite simple: most of us have more control over our anger than we think we do.

ANGER CAN BE HABIT-FORMING

What appears to be happening in Hilda's family is something that is quite common. Children get into the habit of using their anger to get what they want. If parents easily acquiesce, children learn that anger is a very effective means for them to get their way. Their anger is reinforced.

Whether the anger is a "Sore Subject" with roots in family dysfunction, marital discord, temperament, or modelling behavior, it becomes a habit through reinforcement; our actions are reinforced by others or by things in the environment. If children throw tantrums to get what they want and succeed in getting their way, the tantrum gets reinforced by success. When this happens repeatedly, tantrums or displays of anger are very likely to become the way these children try to assert their wishes—not only with parents, but with others as well.

Gerald Patterson, a well-known researcher on children's behavior, has found that when angry outbursts used in this kind of coercive fashion become a way of life in the family, they often become the chief communication pattern between the child and the world in general. Needless to say, this usually leads to many problems for that young person—many of which continue throughout adulthood.

I'm not saying that children can always control their anger or that parents should always use $20 bills to get them to do so. Rather, I simply want to alert you to the fact that, in most cases, anger is more controllable than most people think—something you need to know in order to apply the strategies that I outline later on.

But, controllable or not, it's helpful to understand the underlying mechanisms in the brain that deal with anger.

ANGRY TYPE A's

We all know people whom we just accept as having bad tempers. In my view, there must be some underlying reason why these individuals have difficulty controlling their impulses. Or perhaps these people have never learned how to calm themselves down effectively.

People who have been severely physically abused or who have had serious head injuries are also prone to explosive tempers. For those individuals, the brain injury might have damaged the pathways which help control anger. Or, if people have witnessed or been exposed to repeated physical abuse, they may never have learned how to use self-control when angry. (For a discussion of some of the physical and psychological illnesses that affect anger, see Chapter Four.)

TYPE CASTING

There are two different types of anger—*explosive* and what I have come to call *gathering and seething* anger. Most of us have either one or the other "type," but, depending on the situation and level of stress, we may exhibit both.

When individuals are cursed with both types of anger, it might not be so easy for them to control themselves.

Whether temperament, biology, or a combination of the two, these "angry" individuals have more trouble than most of us in controlling that brittle sleeping giant once it is aroused.

Let's review the two types of anger now.

EXPLOSIVE ANGER: FAST AND FURIOUS

Explosive anger builds up very rapidly, erupts, and then subsides. For example:

George, an 8-year-old, gets called a sissy by the youngster sitting next to him in class. George immediately turns around and punches the child in the stomach. By the time George visits the vice-principal 15 minutes later, he is somewhat upset, but no longer explosive. By the time he talks to his parents that evening, he admits he overreacted to the provocation. Three days later in a therapy session, George assures the therapist that he handled his anger and that he won't explode again. But, two days later, when he's shoved in the playground by another child, George trips him. A fight starts and George has to be pulled off of the child by the teacher. Several hours later, George feels upset that he blew up at the child, but he is no longer angry.

George's anger pattern is repeated over and over again— in school and even at home. Although in many situations it is healthy to express anger directly and immediately, in George's case, his anger is out of control. Instead of asserting his displeasure in a constructive way by saying something such as the tried and true "Sticks and stones..." or "Hey, leave me alone!" he reacted explosively and aggressively— which got him into trouble. In essence, we can say that George gets too angry, too easily, and too often.

GATHERING AND SEETHING ANGER: THE STEW AND ITS COLD DESSERT OF REVENGE

Explosive anger is very different from the gathering and seething type of anger. The latter often takes the form of a

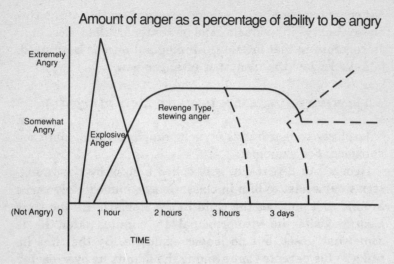

Amount of anger as a percentage of ability to be angry

Graph illustrates course of two different kinds of anger - explosive anger and revenge type anger.
Dotted lines show four possible outcomes. Other outcomes are also possible.

grudge or an outright act of revenge. This sort of anger seems to rise gradually but continues for long periods of time.

The danger with this kind of anger is that it becomes a poison, an obsession, preoccupying people's waking thoughts and sometimes paralyzing them to the extent that they can't perform normal tasks at home or at work. Even children can get consumed by this kind of anger. Take the case of 9-year-old Sarah:

Sarah gets upset one day because the girl next to her is wearing a dress that Sarah's mother refused to buy for her. In addition, Sarah remembers that this same girl criticized her at lunch. She begins to think of ways to get back at her and asks several of her friends to help. Sarah devises a plan to throw all of the girl's books into the sink in the bathroom while the girl is at recess. When the deed is done, the horrified girl goes to the teacher, and Sarah is found out. When she is placed on in-school suspension, Sarah threatens to get even with the girl for telling . . . perpetuating the anger, keeping it alive, destructive and unproductive for all.

In both George and Sarah's cases, we can see that anger is a crippling phenomenon. Getting proper help is vital. If your child exhibits either of these two types of anger, I would suggest that you get counseling for him or her. Many of the suggestions that I will offer later on should prove helpful, but they might not be sufficient for really getting at the root of your child's difficulties.

But, before we can go on to these anger strategies, there is still more to anger than meets the eye. In fact, much of what we know about anger is false. Read on....

CHAPTER THREE

ANGER MYTHS

"If I give my angry child medication, he'll turn into a zombie."
"I guess I'm just not a good enough disciplinarian."
"I don't know what to do when my kid throws a tantrum."
"He won't listen to reason."

These comments come from concerned parents who are trying to cope with their children's hostile behavior.

In the previous chapters, you have learned some of anger's expressions. You've seen how it can take root. But, before I discuss prevention, I'd like to take a few moments to dispel some of anger's myths.

Myth # 1: "My Child's Angry Because He's Just a Bad Seed."

Billy was furious at his schoolmates. He was furious with his parents. He'd stick out his tongue at his teachers. He'd put out his foot to trip someone walking down the street. He was a terror—and it was no surprise that he was suspended from school until further notice.

But when a school psychologist interviewed him, he suspected that Billy was an abused child. He was proved right. Billy's anger had nothing to do with being "bad." It was the only way he knew how to deal with frustration and pain.

Myth # 2: "If My Angry Child Takes Medication, He'll Turn Into a Stranger. He'll Lose All Zest For Life."

Not true. Therapy, sometimes augmented by medication, can help children cope with anger. If a child has a learning disability, that may need remediation. If children have Attention-Deficit Hyperactivity Disorder (ADHD), medication can sometimes help them cope with inattention, distractability and hyperactivity; it can help with the coexisting depression that sometimes accompanies ADHD. Anger can be a symptom for many psychological and physical illnesses—many of which can be helped by evaluation, psychotherapy, and, if indicated, medication. (I'll discuss this in more detail in the next chapter.)

Myth # 3: "My Child's Anger Is All My Fault."

Judy was born a difficult child. She cried almost all the time. She was fidgety and she refused to eat and sleep. Consequently, her parents became frustrated in dealing with her. They tried to be patient, but after many sleepless nights, their patience wore thin.

Unfortunately, Judy's difficult personality stayed with her, reinforced by her parent's irritability. She got into fights at school; she was stubborn and refused to listen to her teachers.

In addition, her conduct was influenced by a speech and reading delay that her teachers did not detect. Judy had difficulty understanding written and spoken words. Her parents tried to help her, but they didn't know what was wrong.

Finally, they brought her to a specialist, who was able to recognize her learning disability and her "difficult" roots—which had little to do with the love and attention her parents gave her.

Yes, Judy's problems became a part of a vicious cycle of anger—but it wasn't solely her parent's fault. Blame heredity, environment, biology, and fate.

These are only a few of the common myths that surround anger and its tantrum-producing, screaming kin. You will most likely discover more misconceptions you'd had as you read on. To help you sift through the myths and find the truth, take a few moments to do this quiz. It will help you see whether anger is a problem in your child—or merely a passing phase.

CHILD QUESTIONNAIRE

CIRCLE THE ANSWER THAT BEST FITS YOUR CHILD:

Home

1. Does the child have temper outbursts at home?
    a. no more than once a month.
    b. no more than once a week.
    c. more than once a week.

2. How does the child handle parental suggestions?
    a. usually accepts suggestions (1–2 times a week).
    b. sometimes accepts suggestions (2–4 times a week).
    c. hardly ever accepts suggestions.

3. With siblings, the child:
    a. rarely hits or yells to get own way (less than once a week).
    b. sometimes hits or yells to get own way (up to once or twice a week).
    c. frequently hits or yells to get own way (2–3 times a week or more).

4. When the child uses his temper to get his/her way, he/she:
   a. rarely gets away with it (less than once a week).
   b. sometimes gets away with it (up to once a week).
   c. frequently gets away with it (at least 1–2 times a week).

5. Over the last six months, the temper outbursts have been:
   a. decreasing.
   b. staying the same.
   c. increasing.

6. When the child has had a rage tantrum or carried out an act of revenge:
   a. no property or physical harm has occurred.
   b. minor damage has occurred (scratches on walls)—no physical injury.
   c. significant property damage or physical injury has occurred.

7. In discussing a previous temper outburst, the child:
   a. learned ways to prevent outbursts over similar issues.
   b. said he learned better ways to handle anger but didn't show it.
   c. showed no ability to learn from temper outbursts.

8. With Friends:
   a. the child's anger has no effect on making friends.
   b. the child's anger makes most friendships end after a short time.
   c. the child's anger prevents friendships from forming.

9. At school, the child's anger:
   a. has no effect on schoolwork or grades.
   b. causes problems with grades and schoolwork in one subject.
   c. causes problems with grades and schoolwork in many subjects.

Other

10. The child's anger:
    a. never results in self-destructive behavior (head banging, injuring arms or legs, or suicidal threats.)
    b. has resulted in threats of self-injury which have not been carried out.
    c. has resulted in physical injury to self and/or suicide attempt.

11. The child:
    a. has never initiated sexual behavior with another child.
    b. has made sexual threats to peers, but has not carried them out.
    c. has sexually acted out with other children.

Scoring

In general:

- Questions 1 through 9: 5 or more b's may suggest sufficient problems with anger to consider a psychological/psychiatric consultation.
- Any b in question 10 or 11 may suggest sufficient issues to consider a psychological/psychiatric consultation.
- Any c in question 1 through 11, especially 10 or 11, may suggest a psychological/psychiatric evaluation.

Of course, an evaluation could be done with lower scores if the parent feels the behavior is escalating or instinctively senses something is seriously awry.

ADOLESCENT QUESTIONNAIRE

Home

1. Does the teenager become abusive and threatening after breaking family rules (like curfew)?
    a. no more than once or twice per year.
    b. at most once a month.
    c. several times per month.

2. How does the teenager deal with responsibilities and chores at home?
    a. usually does chores.
    b. tries to avoid doing chores.
    c. routinely blames others for failure to do chores and/or refuses to do any chores.

3. With siblings, the teenager:
    a. rarely hits or yells to get own way (less than once a week).
    b. sometimes hits or yells to get own way (up to once or twice a week).
    c. frequently hits or yells to get own way (2–3 times a week or more).

4. When the teenager gets angry, parents:
   a. rarely are frightened and feel the need to let the teenager get his own way (less than 1–2 times per year).
   b. sometimes are frightened and feel the need to let the teenager get his own way (up to once or twice every 2–3 months).
   c. often are frightened and feel the need to let the teenager get his own way (more than once per month).

5. Over the last six months, the anger outbursts have been:
   a. decreasing.
   b. staying the same.
   c. increasing.

6. The teenager's anger usually results in:
   a. no property damage or physical injury.
   b. minor property damage (scrapes on the walls)—no physical injury.
   c. significant property damage or physical injury.

7. The teenager's way of coping with disappointment or rejection:
   a. rarely involves "getting even" (up to a few times a year).
   b. sometimes involves "getting even" (up to once per month).
   c. frequently involves "getting even" (at least once per week).

8. In discussing a previous temper outburst, the teenager:
   a. learned ways to prevent outbursts over similar issues.
   b. said that he learned better ways to handle anger but didn't show it.
   c. showed no ability to learn from temper outbursts.

Friends

9. The teenager and his/her friends:
   a. rarely engage in destructive or aggressive behavior (destroying property, getting into fights)—no more than once per year.
   b. sometime engage in destructive or aggressive behavior—several times per year.
   c. frequently engage in destructive or aggressive behavior—once per month or more.

10. The teenager's anger:
    a. has no effect on making friends.
    b. makes most friendships end after a short time.
    c. prevents friendships from forming.

School

11. The teenager's anger:
    a. has no effect on schoolwork or grades.
    b. causes problems with grades and schoolwork in one subject.
    c. causes problems with grades and schoolwork in many subjects.

Other

12. In dealing with anger and frustration, the teenager:
    a. never uses drugs or alcohol.
    b. has used drugs or alcohol in the past but not currently.
    c. uses drugs or alcohol.

13. The teenager's anger:
    a. never results in self-destructive behavior (injuring self or other dangerous behavior like driving at reckless speeds).
    b. has provoked threats of self-injury or reckless behavior or self-destructive behavior which have not been carried out.
    c. has resulted in physical injury to self, reckless behavior or suicide attempt.

14. The teenager:
    a. has never been sexually aggressive with another peer (see Chapter 6).
    b. has made sexual threats to peers, but has not carried them out.
    c. has been sexually aggressive with another peer.

Scoring

In general:
- Questions 1 through 10: 3 or more b's may suggest sufficient issues to consider a psychological/psychiatric consultation.
- Any b in question 12, 13, or 14 alone may suggest sufficient issues to consider a psychological/psychiatric evaluation.
- Any c question 1 through 13, especially 11, 12, 13 or 14, would suggest a reason for a psychological evaluation.

PARENT QUESTIONNAIRE: *Judging Your Own Coping Skills*

1. In conflicts with teenagers or children:
    a. physical force is seldom used (2–3 times per year).
    b. physical force is sometimes used (up to once per month).
    c. physical force is frequently used (up to several times per week).

2. Coming home to be with children or teenagers:
   a. is seldom dreaded (2–3 times per year).
   b. is sometimes dreaded (up to once per month).
   c. is frequently dreaded (several times per week).

3. Children and teenagers:
   a. rarely increase conflicts between parents, including step-parents and noncustodial parents (1–2 times per year).
   b. sometimes increase conflicts between parents, including stepparents and noncustodial parents (1–2 times per month).
   c. frequently increase conflicts between parents, including stepparents and noncustodial parents (more than 1–2 times per month).

4. Conflicts with children and teenagers:
   a. never prompts a parent to take nerve pills or alcoholic drinks.
   b. rarely prompts a parent to take nerve pills or alcoholic drinks (1–2 times per year).
   c. sometimes prompts a parent to take nerve pills or alcoholic drinks (more than 1–2 times per year).

5. To deal with a child/teenager's behavior problems, parents:
   a. are rarely called away from jobs to school or day care (2–3 times per year).
   b. are sometimes called away from jobs to school or day care (up to once per month).
   c. are frequently called away from jobs to school or day care (more than once per month).

6. In dealing with angry outbursts, parents:
   a. have never been physically injured.
   b. have rarely been physically injured (up to once or twice per year).
   c. have sometimes been physically injured (more than once or twice per year).

7. In caring for children or teenagers, parents:
   a. can usually find time each week or two for some adult activities/contacts (1–2 times every 1–2 weeks).
   b. can sometimes find time each week or two for some *adult* activities/contacts (at least once per month).
   c. can rarely find time each week or two for some *adult* activities/contacts (less than once per month.)

8. In dealing with management or child/teenager's negative/
   hostile behavior, parent:
   a. rarely lost control and acted in a manner that he/she
      regretted (3–6 times per year).
   b. sometimes lost control and acted in a manner that he/she
      regretted (0–2 times per month).
   c. often lost control and acted in a manner that he/she regret-
      ted (once a week or more).

9. In dealing with aggressive behavior of a child/teenager, parent's decisions:
   a. are usually accepted (challenged less than once per month).
   b. are often challenged (challenged once per week).
   c. are frequently challenged (challenged more than once per
      week).

10. In dealing with aggressive behavior of a child/teenager, parents:
    a. rarely feel they need professional help (less than once per
       month).
    b. often feel they need professional help (once or twice per
       month).
    c. usually feel they need professional help (at least once per
       week).

Scoring

• Any three b's or any c may mean you should seek psychological/
  psychiatric evaluation to help you deal with your child's anger
  problems.

And, if any of these statements ring true, read on to
discover some of the masks anger wears, as well as specific
strategies to deal with your child's anger safely and
productively.

CHAPTER FOUR

ANGER DISORDERS

- Rose couldn't spend more than ten minutes in her seat. No sooner did she get comfortable at her desk when she'd be off and running around the room, screaming at the top of her lungs, oblivious to her teacher and the other kids.
- Sammy would come home from school without a word of greeting. He'd grab a bottle of juice, head up the stairs, and go into his room. He'd slam the door and, five minutes later, the music would be blaring. But just try to knock on the door to ask him a question. He'd start roaring at you—and throw things at his closed door.
- Melinda was a quiet, gentle child—until that fateful day she went out for a bicycle ride. She wasn't wearing a helmet because no one wore helmets. She liked the feel of the wind on her hair. But that morning was very bright. The sun hit her eyes. She didn't see the pothole. Fifteen-year-old Melinda fell and hit her head. When she came out of a coma several days later, she'd become violent, aggressive, and very, very angry.

These children are angry—but not because they feel that particular emotion as a response to injustice or rejection.

Rose has ADHD. Sammy is depressed. And Melinda had a brain injury.

Anger has many faces, many moods—and can be a symptom of many disorders. Let's briefly go over some of these "painful expressions" now:

Painful Expression # 1: Behavior Disorders

I treated a 12-year-old boy with a history of running away from school, stealing, lying, and getting into fights. He also had been caught breaking into homes and setting fires. These specific behaviors are what define a *conduct disorder*—and anger is no stranger to its victims.

Two others disorders that have anger as their chief feature are *intermittent explosive disorder* and *oppositional defiant disorder*. In the former, frequent outbursts of temper prevent the child from functioning normally. In the latter, the child:

- Has a generally defiant attitude toward all authority
- Frequently argues with adults, refusing to comply with their requests
- Is often touchy
- Can be easily annoyed by others
- Is angry and resentful
- Becomes possibly spiteful or vindictive
- Might habitually blame others for his mistakes
- Might swear frequently or use obscene language

"SEEING RED"
A Person with Intermittent Explosive Disorder
- May develop it at any age
- Has explosive anger outbursts that are not justified by outside events
- Has no other behavioral problems
- Does not have any other underlying psychiatric illness, including psychosis or manic-depressive disease

---

It is important for you to be aware of these behavior disorders so that you can get the proper help for your child if he suffers from one of them. The strategies that I will offer in later chapters may not be as effective unless these underlying disorders are concurrently treated by a professional.

Painful Expression # 2: Mood Disorders

When people are depressed, they are often angry—either at themselves or at others. But working with the anger itself is likely to do little to alleviate the depression. Sometimes angry and depressed people also have conduct disorders. In these cases, a therapist will have to work with both the depression and the conduct disorder to improve the person's problem with anger.

People who have manic-depressive disease have extreme mood swings. They are often angry, particularly in the high or manic phase. But, again, one must treat the underlying psychiatric illness, not the anger, in order to improve the person's condition.

Painful Expression # 3: Psychotic or Thought Disorders

Anger can also be a feature of people with psychotic disorders. For example, Allen, a 17-year-old patient of mine, began to think that people were reading his mind and that television was sending special messages to him. He thought he was bad and that other people were poisoning his mind. In class, he had a lot of difficulty concentrating, and he'd often get angry at others when they asked him even simple questions.

Treating or confronting this young man about his anger would do nothing to ameliorate the psychotic illness he had. But psychiatric treatment of the illness itself should improve the way he perceived the world and thus dissipate his anger.

"SEEING RED"
Facts about Childhood and
Adolescent Depression

- Depression is much less common before puberty
- Experts are unsure if childhood depression is the same as adult depression
- The best way to find out if children or teenagers are depressed is to observe their behavior and to ask questions.
- Symptoms may include irritability, withdrawal, decreased energy, crying spells, sleeping and eating disturbances
- Asking the right questions may reveal hopelessness, loss of energy, thoughts of self-harm, and lack of pleasure in life
- Anxiety, worry, and fear of abandonment may accompany depression as a second disorder
- Depression may be combined with alcohol, marijuana, and drug abuse problems
- Depression may be present from childhood through adulthood, chronically or episodically

---

Painful Expression # 4: Chemical Dependency

When people are using drugs or alcohol, their underlying anger is often exacerbated. In addition, some individuals can only show their anger when under the influence of a chemical substance. Whichever it is, the anger and the chemical dependency must both be worked on in therapy for the person to improve. (However, if anger only manifests "under the influence," abstinence alone may eliminate the problem.)

Treatment of chemical dependency should be conducted

by a therapist with specific training in this specialty. By the same token, inpatient treatment should be at a facility specifically geared to treat this disorder.

Painful Expression # 5: Personality Disorders or Styles

Children under 18 years old are usually not thought to have personality disorders. Character traits, however, are often present in young people.

In the paranoid type of personality disorder, an individual usually has an angry disposition that is coupled with a marked suspiciousness of others. Or, if people are characterized as narcissistic, they may be intensely overinvolved with themselves. If people are passive-aggressive, they will be somewhat devious in dealings with others, particularly those in authority, and will often show their anger in covert ways, that they may disown when confronted about it.

Young people who are developing borderline personality characteristics show a tendency to act out their impulses in search of an identity. The ways in which they act out may include explosive behavior, substance abuse, sexually provocative behavior, and antisocial behavior.

I mention these different personality disorders because they can have anger as a component. And, like the other disorders, treatment of this anger must be approached within the context of the underlying disorder first. If you have any suspicion that your child has one of these personality disturbances, you may wish to have him or her evaluated professionally.

Painful Expression # 6: Medical Illness

Certain medical illnesses are accompanied by irritability and anger. For example, a patient of mine once developed a fever, cough, and rash. Over several hours she became increasingly irritable, angry, and argumentative. In this

"SEEING RED"
Sexually Aggressive Behavior is
Defined by Two Conditions

1. The perpetrator has power over a victim because he (usually) is stronger, older, and more verbal. In addition, he has a position of authority (counselor, sitter, etc.), an intimidating manner, and, possibly, a weapon.
2. The victim has reason to fear for him or herself if he/she refuses the perpetrator's demands.

Sexually aggressive behavior is often aggravated, but not caused, by drugs and alcohol.

Obscene phone calls, voyeurism, stealing a victim's clothes, being verbally hostile and profane, and touching or fondling when the victim is asleep, are all examples of sexually aggressive behavior.

Sexually aggressive behavior may be present at any age. It often begins by age 12 or 13.

case, her pediatrician diagnosed encephalitis—an infection of the nervous system. Thus, infection of the nervous system can cause changes in mood and personality.

Painful Expression # 7: Epilepsy

Anger can be a feature in some types of epilepsy. Temporal lobe epilepsy, for example, is caused by abnormal activity in the temporal lobe(s) of the brain; a form of electrical discharge in this same area has been associated with anger.

In one case I know of, a 16-year-old boy known to have an explosive temper became enraged and tried to strangle a classmate who taunted him. After the incident, he blacked out and didn't remember it. But an electroencephalogram revealed the kind of abnormal activity in the temporal lobe that indicates he suffered from a seizure. Like the chicken and the egg, however, it's not always clear whether the seizure triggers the anger or vice versa.

Other seizure disorders, such as grand mal epilepsy, may also be present in individuals with explosive tempers. Grand mal seizures are characterized by periods of unconsciousness and motor movements of the body. They might also include partial seizures in which the person experiences electric discharges in local areas of his brain that translate into specific body movements or behaviors.

Professor Michael Rutter's Isle of Wight study found that individuals with epilepsy and other neurological disorders are five times more likely to have psychiatric problems than the general population. Therefore, it is sometimes very useful in the evaluation of children with explosive tempers to have them undergo a "sleep-deprived electroencephalogram." Keeping them up all night and increasing the brain's irritability factor also increases the likelihood of a more accurate diagnosis. In our hospital alone, we have had six or seven children whose routine electroencephalograms were normal. But when sleep-deprived, the same test showed evidence of temporal lobe or partial seizure activity.

Painful Expression # 8: Brain Damage

Brain damage can mean many things. For our purposes, we will say that people are brain-damaged when they exhibit some evidence of brain abnormality from either a sophisticated diagnostic X-ray, such as a CAT scan or MRI scan, an electroencephalogram, or a thorough neurological exam.

Brain damage can have many causes. It can be the result of an infection, such as encephalitis, or the result of traumatic injury from a fall, blow to the head, or gunshot wound. In addition, there are individuals with brain damage for which the cause is unknown.

Not everybody who is brain-damaged has temper problems. However, brain damage can promote both impulsive and aggressive behavior.

Hector, 15, was in a BB shooting accident. X-rays indicated that a BB had lodged in the temporal area of his brain, but had not produced any clear defects. However, Hector began to exhibit a lot of anger, grabbing people and hitting them without provocation. Prior to his injury, he had done none of these things.

Painful Expression # 9:
Attention-Deficit Hyperactivity Disorder

Attention-deficit hyperactivity disorder (ADHD) is one of the most common psychiatric diagnoses associated with anger. Those with this disorder tend to be impulsive, destructive, and hyperactive. Some of them are also assaultive and aggressive.

Eight-year-old Jimmy is typical of children with ADHD and behavior problems. For several years, Jimmy had trouble sitting still and staying in his seat at school. He fidgeted a lot, often grabbing, punching, and shoving other kids who sat next to him. After being treated with Ritalin, sometimes an effective drug for this disorder, his distractibility, impulsivity, hyperactivity, and angry outbursts all diminished.

Ritalin isn't always effective in ADHD. In some individuals, the hyperactivity diminishes, but the aggressiveness stays the same. In these cases, other stimulants, such as Dexedrine and Cylert, antidepressants, and antihypertensive medications, such as Catapres (Generic Name: Clonidine), have been used successfully. (I'll discuss medication in more detail in Chapter Eight.)

Painful Expression # 10: Tourette's Syndrome

Tics are the most outstanding feature of Tourette's Syndrome. Hyperactivity and aggression are also common with this disorder. And it's also not uncommon for its victims to utter profanities.

Sometimes treating the disorder with drugs such as Catapres helps to decrease the angry outbursts. But I am not aware of any long-term studies that show how effective this drug is in alleviating accompanying aggression.

Painful Expression # 11:
Panic Disorders and Phobias

Individuals with tempers may sometimes suffer from panic disorders and phobias as well. Their anger might be exacerbated when they are in a phobic situation—whether it is being forced into an elevator, going outside the house, or getting caught in a crowd. In these cases, antidepressants and antianxiety medication can treat the panic, the phobic feelings, and the unsettling anger.

Painful Expression # 12: Depression

In the 1960s, it was commonly believed that angry feelings and assaultive behavior were often symptoms of an underlying undiagnosed depression. The theory suggested that the angry behavior would cease if the depression was treated with therapy or drugs. Consequently, during the past twenty years, antidepressants have been widely prescribed for aggressive children and adolescents.

But the results haven't been clearcut. Even when the depression improved, the aggressive behavior sometimes remained. *Not everyone who is aggressive is depressed.* Anger can be caused by a wide range of psychological, neurological, or physiological factors. It can also be a learned behavior. Antidepressants do not address any of these issues.

Current research suggests that when depression and behavior problems co—exist, they are two different disorders— usually a combination of conduct problems and depression. The same thing can be said when depression is seen with individuals who have panic disorder, obsessive-compulsive disorder, and attention-deficit hyperactivity disorder.

Under these circumstances, treating the depression alone, as I noted above, will not usually eliminate the anger. But reducing the depression *can* motivate the individual to work on aggressive feelings. Therefore, therapy and antidepressants can sometimes be seen as a first step—rather than the ultimate treatment—for individuals whose depression is accompanied by another disorder.

Painful Expression # 13: Manic Depressive Disease

One patient, 15-year-old Louise, was considered "hyper" by her family and friends. She had intense mood swings for days at a time, during which she'd be energetic to the point of being overbearing and aggressive. These "highs" would be followed by periods of withdrawal, crying spells, and expressions of hopelessness. A diagnosis of manic-depressive illness was made by her psychiatrist, and she was placed on lithium carbonate. On this medication, her depression diminished along with her angry episodes.

Manic-depressive disease is very difficult to diagnose in children and adolescents. Further, some recent studies suggest that manic-depressive disease in children is often resistant to treatment with lithium, the most common drug used for this disease in adults. Nevertheless, lithium carbonate, as Louise's example shows, can be helpful and should be tried if anger is a problem and manic-depressive illness is suspected. In some cases, it can also diminish anger in children and teens who show no evidence of the disease.

Painful Expression # 14: Mental Retardation

Some children suffering from mental retardation exhibit explosive behavior. Under these circumstances, the anger needs to be evaluated neurologically and psychologically to

---

"SEEING RED"
Juvenile Bipolar or Manic-Depressive
Illness Is...

...very difficult to diagnose because it can often seem like a behavior disorder or ADHD. It can be characterized by:

- Mood Swings
- Irritability
- Hyperactivity
- Poor social skills
- Alcohol, marijuana, and drug abuse

Age: May be present from childhood. Adult onset bipolar disease usually begins after age 25.

---

screen for the presence of co-existing disorders, such as temporal lobe epilepsy and hyperactivity. Treating the underlying biological cause of the anger, if possible, while at the same time employing the behavioral strategies I will outline later, may alleviate some of the aggressive acting out. I also recommend seeking professional help.

Painful Expression # 15: Sleep Disorders

Though it's rare, some sleep disorders do produce explosive behavior. For instance, individuals who sleepwalk can become quite agitated when interrupted. And, sometimes, those who have disturbed sleep patterns can have angry outbursts in the middle of the night.

Jeremy, a 14-year-old patient, had been severely physically abused as a child. When he entered therapy and began to work on behavioral problems, he began to have nightmares about past assaults he had endured. In addition, in the middle of the night, he would wake up and throw things; he would scream, yell, and become more and more violent if anyone tried to guide him back to bed.

I felt that Jeremy had what is known as a "Stage Three Sleep Disorder," so I prescribed a minor tranquilizer, Klonopin, for a brief time period. This proved effective in eliminating the explosive nightmare episodes. If you suspect your child or adolescent has a sleep disorder like Jeremy, have the child evaluated by someone who specializes in this area.

These words of advice are true for any of the "Painful Expressions" I've briefly discussed in this chapter. Specialists can pinpoint problem behavior. And, because they are more familiar with the disorder, they know exactly what treatment will work—and how it progresses.

But recovery does begin at home. And there is much you, as parents, can do to help your angry child. Read on....

CHAPTER FIVE

HOW CHILDREN GET ANGRY

Anger has many causes. A child's home life, physical and mental condition, and peer relationships contribute to his being angry. Being aware of these many forces is a crucial step in understanding and helping your child to control anger more effectively. I've divided my discussion into two separate chapters: one on children's anger and the other on adolescents' anger, because these two age groups live in different worlds with different concerns.

REALISTIC VS. UNREALISTIC

One of the first things you should do in assessing your child's anger is to try to determine whether or not it is realistic. For example, I know of a 6-year-old child who threw a 45-minute tantrum when he learned that a snow day was canceled. The child expressed the fear that there would never be a snow day again.

In dealing with children, the parents have to realize that because of children's developmental level, they have difficulty imagining the future. In order to help a child cope with this situation, the parents would do well to reassure the child that there will probably be other snow days in the future. The parents have to help the child see reality more clearly.

On the other hand, a child's angry reaction might indeed be very realistic, but spring from events in the immediate past of which the parent may be unaware. For example, I treated a 9-year-old patient who became extremely upset when she noticed her brother playing with one of her stuffed toys. She screamed and yelled at him, then ran into her room and slammed the door.

On the surface, this might seem to be an exaggerated response to a minor incident. If you knew more about the child's view of the situation, you would see that she had valid reasons for being angry. In the first place, she was afraid of her brother because he was bigger. She was also upset because he had gone into her room without permission and, most likely, looked at other items she valued. In addition, she really treasured that stuffed animal and feared that her brother would tear it up as he had some of his own toys.

If they wanted to help this girl with her realistic anger, her parents would have to be aware of all the contributing factors. Although reassurances would be important, it would also be necessary to make changes in her brother's behavior—perhaps limiting his access to her room and to her toys.

In other words, if a child's anger is realistic, the elements that caused that anger will have to be modified if you don't want that anger to reoccur.

THE THREE C'S OF ANGER

In uncovering the reasons behind children's anger, it can be helpful to pinpoint whether or not they are using it as a way to cope, as a defense mechanism in order to conceal (or protect) themselves, or as a copying device, imitating another person's angry behavior.

COPING

If a young child is teased about his puppy's recent death and he reacts angrily by throwing things at the taunting child, we can say that his anger is his way of coping with the loss of his pet.

Even though he knows he is helpless, that he cannot do anything to bring his pet back, when he gets angry at someone else, he has the feeling that, at least, he is doing something.

But loss is only one area where a child might use anger to cope. Another traumatic situation in which a child might use anger to cope is that of sexual or physical abuse.

I treated a child who was being physically abused by her parents and had scars and bruises on her legs from their beatings. When she became increasingly belligerent and irritable, her teacher talked to her and discovered that the child had been sworn to secrecy by her parents; they said that if she told anyone about the abuse, they (the parents) would be sent to jail. When other children began to tease her about her family, she yelled back at them, saying that what her family did to her was her business and no one was going to make fun of them.

This girl is not alone. Abused children often assume a belligerent stance when trying to cope with their trauma. They take on the view of their parents: It is not the family who is dangerous, but the outside world—where the powers-that-be would split the family up if it became known what they were doing.

CONCEALING, OR PROTECTING

Sometimes children use anger to protect what they are doing. For example, Jonas, age 8, got angry and ran away when his teacher confronted him about giving away donuts to other kids at recess. When the teacher told Jonas's mother, she discovered that five dollars was missing from her purse. When both the teacher and his mother confronted Jonas, he again got extremely angry—but he also broke down into tears, saying that he had no friends and that he took his mother's money and bought the donuts to try and win some friends.

In this case, Jonas' anger is an attempt to divert his teacher and his mother from questioning him further about what had happened. It is a smokescreen to hide his stealing—and to protect him from having to admit the painful fact that he is unable to make friends.

Sometimes "protecting anger" serves the purpose of distracting others from behavior the individual wants kept concealed. For example, a young girl is one of six children in her family. She is older than the other children and she likes to stay up late. One of the ways she has learned to do so is to start yelling and screaming right around bedtime. The other children join in, and by the time her frazzled parents calm everyone down, a half hour has passed. Thus, the girl's anger has served as a ploy in getting her to stay up later than her parents intended.

Anger can be used protectively as a release from another, perhaps more painful, emotion. For example, if a child is frustrated at not being able to do the math problems in class one day, he might explode in anger and throw the book on the floor; he might say the book is too hard and that he didn't want to learn how to do the problems anyway. Instead of expressing his feelings of inadequacy, he has chosen the shortcut of exploding in anger and blaming his failure on the book.

COPYING

As I noted in Chapter One, children's expressions of anger are often a direct result of something that has been done to them. When this occurs, we say that they are copying.

Henrietta, a 10-year-old patient of mine, told me how, one day, she noticed that the girl sitting next to her had a blue ribbon in her hair that everyone was admiring. Henrietta very much wanted to have the ribbon, so she screamed at the child to give it to her. When the girl said, "No," Henrietta grabbed it and said, "If you ever want to see this again, you'd better not tell anybody I took it."

In this example, Henrietta chose screaming, yelling, and intimidation to try to get what she wanted. When questioned, she admitted that she copied this behavior from her older sister—who always managed to take Henrietta's things in this manner. Though there are probably other forces at work here as well, copying seems to be the major factor in her behavior.

SIFTING THROUGH THE MANY SOURCES OF ANGER

Once you understand how children use anger for the three "C's" of coping, concealing (or protecting), and copying, you can begin to analyze how each might be present, alone or in combination, in your own child's behavior.

The following example contains elements of both protecting and coping:

Eight-year-old Franklin has been very angry since his teammate, Ralph, hit him with a ball at recess. He remembers all the things Ralph has done to him over the past few months, and he continues to seethe about this. After recess one day, he slips a handful of mud into Ralph's lunchbox. When caught, he reacts angrily.

Franklin's anger protects him by covering up his guilt and embarrassment at getting caught. He also uses revenge as a way of coping with his own feelings of humiliation in the past, thanks to Ralph. He wanted to "get even."

WHEN SOMEONE ELSE DOES THE WORK: SETUPS

Sometimes individuals don't feel like expressing their own anger directly. Instead, they provoke someone else, who then serves as an outlet for their emotions, a sort of substitute receptacle for anger.

Timothy has a reputation for exploding easily—and other children often exploit this. One afternoon, while he was sitting in the Little League dugout with the rest of the team, another boy, Thomas, chewed some gum and blew a big bubble in his face. Timothy, in turn, hit Thomas. When questioned, Thomas admitted that he was angry at Timothy for always getting to bat in front of him and for bragging about being a better hitter. Rather than take the "flak," he provoked Timothy into a fight—getting what he wanted without the blame. This is a classic example of a "setup." It illustrates how having an explosive temper can make an individual vulnerable to exploitation by others.

GETTING NOTICED THROUGH ANGER: NEGATIVE ATTENTION

If their positive behavior doesn't get rewarded or noticed sufficiently, sometimes children resort to anger, a basic negative behavior, to get their parents to pay attention to them. I have a 9-year-old patient whose behavior is a classic example of this. It seems that Isabella's parents spend so much time disciplining her and her three siblings that they forget to tell them they appreciate it when one of them is well-behaved. This kind of parenting can make children feel neglected; it can force them into negative attention-seeking behaviors. It's as though negative attention is preferable to no attention at all.

JUST A BEGINNING

Of course, there are many other reasons for children's anger, but, hopefully, this chapter can act as a springboard, opening your eyes to the possibility that there is more than just the surface tantrum involved. Deciding if children are using anger to cope, conceal (or protect), or copy, or any combination thereof, can be the first step in getting to the root of what is really bothering them. Determining if they are acting realistic or unrealistic, if they are "setting you up" or trying to get your attention in negative ways, can help open the door for a fruitful dialogue—which, in turn, makes children more open to the strategies in the next chapter.

CHAPTER SIX

WAYS TO HELP CHILDREN WITH ANGER

Being able to let others know we have angry feelings in a constructive way is important to our psychological health and self-esteem. But, as we all know, this is easier said than done. Most people never learned the right way to express anger from their parents or other role models—who never learned it from their parents, and so on and so on. . . .

As a result, many people use anger in ways that are hurtful to themselves or others. Unfortunately, those who do this consistently are almost certain to have serious problems getting along in life.

ANGER'S GOLDEN RULE:
A PERSON MUST CONTROL ANGER TO
EXPRESS IT PROPERLY

It's true. Control is the key—as paradoxical as this might appear. For proper, healthy expression, anger must not only be recognized, but harnessed and controlled. This doesn't mean squelching your anger completely—or even denying that it's there. Such suppression of anger usually doesn't work. The anger comes out in indirect, but still damaging, ways, such as sarcasm, backstabbing, self-destructive behavior, and even perhaps psychosomatic illness.

Mature adults who use their anger productively know that they don't even have to raise their voices to let their feelings be known. Communicating one's displeasure in a calm manner with well-chosen words will almost always produce better results than emotional tirades. They find relief by discussing their feelings with a friend or spouse, by taking a walk around the block, or through some similarly satisfying outlet.

But mature, healthy adults begin life as children. It's vital that you teach your child the proper way to express anger. It's up to you to help stop a legacy of inappropriate anger from becoming a way of life for your child—and yourself. To that end, I am going to explain certain steps you can follow to help your child get control of that irritable giant within—"spare the rod" strategies that are an important part of what those in the social sciences call the socialization process. These steps will help your child deal better with stressful emotional and social situations.

"Spare the Rod" Strategy # 1: Understanding

You first have to understand a problem before you can change it. Knowing what's behind your child's anger is the important first step in offering help toward that change.

Here's an example: Nine-year-old Stephanie had a screaming fit. She threw her hairbrush when her mother told her to wear a specific outfit to school the next day. After Stephanie calmed down, she told her mother that several kids in class had teased a girl who wore clothes similar to the ones Stephanie's mother had chosen for her. As a result, she was afraid that she, too, would be teased if she wore them.

By getting at the root of her daughter's outburst, Stephanie's mother was able to defuse her anger and increase understanding between the two of them. But what if her daughter behaves the same way, throwing the hairbrush and screaming, if she becomes distressed again? In this case, Stephanie's mother might be justified in wondering if talk alone was sufficient. When a maladaptive pattern of coping with distress does start to develop, I advise parents that it's time for a more intensive approach—which leads to other "Spare the Rod" strategies.

"Spare the Rod" Strategy # 2: Tackling a Temper at Home

If you have a child who has temper problems, and if you know the reason for it, what do you do?

Lets examine Larry's situation:

Larry has been having explosive episodes for three to four years. In addition to angry outbursts, he has destroyed his 6-year-old brother's toys, threatened to run away from home, and has refused to do what is asked of him. The family has attempted to cope with this by spanking him, sending him to his room, and screaming at him.

All these approaches have failed.

Worse, Larry is beginning to have problems at school. He has been sent to the vice principal twice during the last month for fighting during recess.

Larry has a problem: at home, at school, and in social situations.

In order to understand a child, like Larry, who has a problem with anger, I usually advise parents to approach his home, school, and social situations (or time spent with friends) separately. Since parents have the most control over what happens at home, they should begin with what happens there. Often, when a child learns to control his temper at home, he learns to cope in other situations as well. Quite simply, controlling anger begins at home.

"Spare the Rod" Strategy # 3: Wait Until the Storm Has Passed

When a child's temper problems start adversely affecting the family, the first thing parents should do is discuss this with him when he has calmed down, when all of you can talk in a more rational manner. The purpose of this discussion is to understand:

1. What is making the child angry?
2. How is the child showing anger?

During the course of this dialogue, parents should try to determine whether the child's anger is realistic or unrealistic. If it's unrealistic, they can help the child see things more clearly. If it is realistic, they can be sympathetic. They can try to find solutions to help alleviate the sources of the anger and pain. When the discussion is over, parents might then say something to the effect that, "We understand why you feel angry, but we want to help you learn how to express it in a less hurtful way. You can tell us that you are angry without getting so out of control."

"Spare the Rod" Strategy # 4: Role-Playing

Once constructive talk between parent and child has become a pattern, it's helpful to try to get children to see how their anger appears to other people. John Lockman at Duke University has pointed out that angry people usually underestimate the impact of their anger on others. They also overestimate the aggressive nature of their victim's remarks. In other words, when people are angry, they tend to discount and minimize how others are affected by their anger. At the same time, they tend to see the limits that other people set as arbitrary, unreasonable, and far more confrontational than they really are.

For this reason, it often helps to ask angry children how they think others are affected by their anger. Sometimes role-playing may be more effective than talking. For example, when Larry's mother asks him how he thinks his anger affects others, he shrugs his shoulders. So she says, "Well, Larry, then let me play you and you play me. Let's say we are at the dinner table." With this, Larry's mother begins screaming at him, "Please hand over the pizza!"

Larry smiles and is somewhat taken aback. He insists, "I couldn't have been that bad!"

"Spare the Rod" Strategy # 5: Rewarding Control

Once children have been confronted with the way they come across when angry, the next step is to discuss how much they think they can control their anger. It has amazed me how often children say that they can control their angry outbursts. If you said, "If I gave you a hundred dollars when you were screaming just then, could you have stopped?" In my experience, most children would say, "Yes, I think so. Where is the hundred dollars?"

This discussion is not designed to make children think that you are going to give them money not to be angry. Rather, it is a way to open their eyes to the fact that they do indeed have more control over their anger than they probably thought. Although I don't advocate paying children to control their anger, I have found that it is effective to reward them in some meaningful way during those confrontations when their anger can still be held in check. In order to employ this reinforcement consistently and effectively, I have devised a method I call the "Donut Test."

Essentially the "Donut Test" is a way to reward children for controlling their anger. In order to be effective, you and your child have to select something of value, some goodie or "donut" that will reinforce the child's positive behavior. After you have discussed the fact that the child probably has more control over his anger than he or she realizes, you might say, "Let's choose something that you like and the

The Donut* Test
(Or a way to assess if a
tantruming child is out-of-control.)

1.

Approach screaming child.

2.

Ask child if he/she would like a donut.
(Hold donut to show child.)

3.

If child says "Yes," then instruct the child as
follows: "I will give you a donut if you get up
and end the angry outburst."

| Child ends angry outburst, Positive Donut Test. Outburst was partly manipulative. | Child does not end angry outburst, Negative Donut Test. Child was out-of-control. |

*"Donut" is the generic reference to an immediate behavioral
reinforcer. The reinforcer varies from child to child. Sweets
are commonly applied reinforcers in this test.

next time you have an angry outburst or tantrum, we'll see if you can stop it and get your reward."

The sort of rewards that I have found most helpful are 15 to 20 minutes of Nintendo time, a food item, such as a donut, or simply some time alone with a parent. If this is beginning to sound like a bribe, let me repeat that the Donut Test is just a way to make children aware that they do have control over their anger. Once that has been established, there is no need to continue the test. It is merely an introduction to the other steps which I will explain later.

In Larry's case, he was offered a "donut" of Super Mario Nintendo for 15 minutes when he began throwing his brother's toys. The "donut" stopped him in his tracks, presenting a clear message to both Larry and his mother that he had more control over his anger than it had first appeared. At this point, the Donut Test achieved several purposes:

- It introduced Larry to the idea that his temper is basically his problem and that he must work to control it himself.
- It showed Larry that, with effort he could control his anger, and the process, although not an easy one, works.
- It helped reduce Larry's mother's stress—by alleviating the erroneous belief that she is the one who has to control her son's temper.

"Spare the Rod" Strategy # 6:
When the Donut Leaves a Hole

What about children who have a negative "Donut Test," who cannot control their temper for the reward they have selected? In times like these, you should broach another discussion about the reward. Maybe the reward the child chose has lost its appeal. In this case, the child should choose another reward.

If such discussions don't work, it's possible that the child is not able to control the outbursts because of biological or organic factors. In this case, the child will require special help before the reward system will work. Neurological evaluation and, possibly, medication might need to be introduced before the Donut test can be used successfully.

But if biological or organic factors are not involved, it's possible the Donut Test didn't take because the child's temper tantrum went too far before you interrupted it. In *The Other 23 Hours*, author Albert E. Trieschman suggested that there are specific stages in a temper tantrum, and in the later ones, they indeed may be out of control. In this case, you would want to try offering the reward earlier on in the process.

However, for some children, the goal of controlling their tempers is too vague and the Donut Test is insufficient. But don't despair. There is still help. In these cases, I have a few other "Spare the Rod" strategies that can help improve a child's impulse control. *Please note: Of course, each of the steps I outline below should be discussed beforehand with the child when he or she is calm and agreeable to talk.*

"Spare the Rod" Strategy # 7: Time Outs

This is not permission to start shooting a few baskets or turn on the TV during football season. Rather, it's an effective device to calm down "out of control" children. When children begin to get angry, they should be asked to take a "time out." Many families use chairs or rooms as places for children to do this. We have also found carpet squares to be helpful. I was first introduced to the use of carpet squares, bath mat size, in my work with Jean Mannino, Ph.D., at the San Diego County Child Inpatient Unit. Carpet squares have the advantage of being small and safe to use. In order for children to sit on the carpet square, they have to have some control over their bodies. Body control is one of the ways children can prove to themselves and to others that they are trying to control their anger.

Here's how our carpet square "time outs" work:

1. First of all comes location. I find it best to position the carpet in hallways or in the kitchen because, when children are trying to get control of themselves in the midst of an angry episode, it is helpful for them to see adults nearby.
2. We ask children to place all of their limbs within the boundaries of the carpet.
3. Once the children are settled on the carpet square, an ordinary baking timer is set for three minutes. Children are then told that if they can control their temper for three minutes, they will be allowed off the carpet square.
4. At the end of three minutes, if the child is still screaming, yelling, or even refusing to sit down, the timer is set for another three minutes.
5. The timer is set yet again if the child continues to act out.
6. It is important when following these steps *not* to get involved in arguments regarding whether the child deserves to be put on the carpet square or, indeed, any other extraneous subject. Focus only on the child's need to sit on the carpet square before pursuing any further discussion.

Overall, most children are able to calm themselves down within three to six minutes—although some children require more time. Once a child is calm, the next step can begin.

"Spare the Rod" Strategy # 8:
Working Through the Tantrum or Angry Outburst—
Analyzing and Processing the Angry Facts

It is critical in working with angry children to review how it all began. Getting children to see why they get angry and how they show it is done through a series of discussions called "processing." It can simply begin with the question, "How did this happen?"

This processing technique should be used once children have calmed down, but is still settled on the carpet square. It is an important part of the "time out" strategy.

"SEEING RED"
Not Too Much of a Good Thing

One of the major advantages of the "time out" carpet squares and processing procedures is that they can be repeated many times in the same day, if needed. Other forms of punishment, like spanking, cannot be frequently repeated because there is a limit to how many times one can be physical with children before one has crossed the line into abuse.

Sending children to their rooms for long periods of time is also difficult to repeat because there are only so many hours in a day. In addition, "banishing" children to their rooms removes them from the family so that they cannot be observed; it eliminates the opportunity to process with them what has been undesirable about their behavior.

Don't be discouraged. If you start the processing and your child starts getting agitated, an additional three minutes on the carpet square might be all that's necessary.

When you repeatedly use the carpet square and the processing technique with a child, you are likely to begin to see a pattern in what drives the child to angry outbursts. Such things as name-calling, jealousy, and feeling threatened are common themes that tend to emerge. Spotting them gives you the opportunity to relate one tantrum to a previous one when discussing it with the child. This helps the child learn from previous mistakes.

For example, you might say: "Do you remember the last time your sister called you 'stupid' at the dinner table? You blew up and had to take 'time out.' Well, tonight you and your brother were calling each other names just before you blew up. It looks like name-calling upsets you."

After your speech, you might stop and ask your child what he or she thinks. If the child agrees with your statement, you might then say, "Well, it still looks like name-calling is one of the things that makes you lose your temper. Maybe you need to plan what else you can do if someone calls you a name."

At this point, children might make their own suggestions. If not, you could offer suggestions, advising children to, say, walk away, count to ten, ignore what is being said, or take "time out" on their own. You might even suggest that the child come to you to talk over the angry feelings.

Once you've had this discussion, it is often helpful to suggest that children draw a picture or even make a tape recording describing the temper tantrum or angry episode. In this way, children take some responsibility for describing and, hopefully, controlling their behavior. When the picture or tape is completed and the child has relayed it to you, "time out" can end and the child can return to regular activities.

This whole process sequence, including settling down on the carpet square, should not take more than 15 minutes.

"Spare the Rod" Strategy # 9: Mealtime Feedback

As a further support for temper control, you can use the family meal as a time to reinforce and encourage your child's efforts. You might point out that controlling feelings is as difficult as doing schoolwork. When Larry, in our example, gave a report at dinner on how he was doing in school, he was also encouraged to tell his parents how he was doing with his temper control. One night, he said, "Well, I took a 'time out' on my own before dinner." Another time, in between bites of baked potato, he said, "I ignored it when my brother called me a name."

Praising a child for these types of statements should serve to strengthen the desire to control his anger.

"SEEING RED"
To Hold or Not to Hold

Should you hold children down on the carpet square during a "time out"? In general, it is best not to do this. If you hold children down, they might blame you for being the cause of their outburst. Children often say things like, "You're killing me!" "You're hurting me!" or "Let go of me!"

If a child is sitting all alone on the carpet square, it is going to be hard for the child to say those things. Besides, holding a child on the carpet square requires a lot of energy; some parents will have a difficult time controlling their own tempers when a child is kicking or hitting them.

Often, a discussion of the "time out" procedure before a tantrum takes place subsequently helps a child use the carpet square without being held. However, if your child refuses to make use of the square, or any other element of the program for that matter, a therapy session may be necessary.

Remember, if there is no basic agreement on the child's part that he or she wants help, ultimately *no* behavioral strategy will succeed.

"Spare the Rod" Strategy # 10: Restitution

"Redressing wrongs" is another useful practice in temper control because it gives children the opportunity to experience how others feel about their anger. By repaying the injured party in some small way for the damages that have been incurred, children also take an active part in healing the hurt that they have caused. Along with my colleagues at Appalachian Hall—Jeanne Devaney, Ph.D., Myles Joyce,

Ph.D., and Jon Hetrick—I have found restitution more effective in getting individuals to change their behavior than punishment.

Here's an example: When 7-year-old Sally broke her 5-year-old sister's doll by throwing it at her, she had to do "time outs." Afterward, Sally was asked to help make her sister's bed for three days. She also had to listen to her sister while she discussed how she felt about the broken doll.

Another example: 11-year-old Norman punched his brother in the face after he lost a card game to him. After several "time outs," Norman was required to do restitution by cleaning up his brother's room for three days and to listen to him talk about how he felt when hit.

Restitution, like "time outs," should be presented to children as one of the steps that they will be going through to learn how to manage anger. You might say something to the effect that, "If you injure children or break something of theirs, you owe them something. This is not something that you can pay for with money. You must pay with work."

We have been using restitution at Appalachian Hall for over a year and a half now and we have discovered that you can use it fairly frequently (one to two times a week). We do, however, make it a point to limit restitution to no more than 15 minutes a day and to no more than three days' running for any one act of destruction. We also reserve restitution for those situations when something is broken or when one child physically hurts another.

But nothing is cut and dried. Sometimes a child will manage a "time out" in a processing session, but refuse to do restitution. We handle this by simply saying that the restitution *must* be done—but the child can do it the next day. We have rarely found children who completely resist doing restitution when we give them this brief respite.

Restitution seems to work better than grounding or other restrictions because it is active rather than passive. It helps children experience firsthand what damage their anger has done. In my experience, children learn more from doing than from having things taken away from them.

One final note: Restitution should be used for all the children in the family, not just the child with the temper problem. Why? Because it creates a family ethic that injuries inflicted by siblings will be redressed whenever possible.

"Spare the Rod" Strategy # 11: Choosing the Right Work for Restitution

Introducing the concept of restitution is not enough. You also need to choose the appropriate chore. The most important thing to remember is to pick something that would be of help to the person who is victimized. This might include making a bed, cleaning a room, or doing the dishes. If a parent has been injured, household chores would be particularly appropriate. If it is a sibling, helping him or her take out the garbage or walk the dog might help ease hurt feelings. The idea is to make the restitution meaningful to both the assaultive child *and* the victim. Such things as writing "I'll never do it again" fifty times, making promises, or saying "I'm sorry" have, in our experience, little impact on preventing further outbursts.

"Spare the Rod" Strategy # 12: Learning Empathy Through Words

In Appalachian Hall, each episode of restitution is followed by the aggressor asking the victim how it felt to be hit, to have a toy destroyed, etc. We have found that the victimized child's words often have a powerful effect on the aggressor. One time, a very aggressive child who'd kicked a peer finally broke down after four restitutions and cried. He said, "I didn't want to hurt you." After this episode, the child seldom had to do restitution with that peer again. His aggressive incidents also decreased.

"Spare the Rod" Strategy # 13: Again and Again

It's a fact: in most cases, restitution increases the level of awareness that angry children have about the damage they do. But it doesn't work in a vacuum. All the other "Spare the Rod" strategies must be used as well—and all of them must be repeated before children are able to gain a measure of control over anger. In *The Other 23 Hours*, authors Wineman and Trieschman point out that "again and again" learning—having the same experience over and over again—is the best teacher of social behavior. Fortunately, all the techniques I describe here lend themselves to repetition.

"Spare the Rod" Strategy # 14: When Anger Strikes Outside the Home

As we all know, children often have their angry outbursts in the most inconvenient places: a store, a friend's house, in a park, or any other public setting. In these instances, it may be impossible to use the carpet squares. The best thing to do is to go home and do "time out" on the carpet there. If it s not practical to leave a place immediately, you can still have the child start his "time out" and processing techniques the minute you get home.

However, public outbursts are often habitual—and they might occur despite your best efforts to take the child home and begin "time out." In this case, you can head the incident off by discussing your expectations with your child *before* going out. You can set very specific rules. If he or she won't agree, you simply don't take the child. If, on the other hand, the child agrees, but still has an outburst while you're out in public, you can leave the place where you are and have a makeshift "time out" in the car.

If none of these options work, you might have to seek out professional help. "Time outs" are effective, especially when they are used consistently and repetitively. But they are not foolproof.

"Spare the Rod" Strategy # 15:
When Anger Goes to School

The strategies I've outlined work for an angry child in a home or public place, but what if the child's tantrums or angry outbursts occur at school—and nowhere else?

If this is the case, I suggest you have a meeting with the school's guidance counselor to discuss these "time out" and processing techniques. It's possible that they can be incorporated into the school's program. In addition, the counselor can help determine what is causing the child's anger. A child with temper problems, for example, is often provoked by another child. Here, a few sessions with the guidance counselor for *both* children can often help stop classroom disruptions.

The use of counseling or therapy is an important way of working with children with temper problems at school. "Time out" and processing techniques can be incorporated into many different therapies.

Ultimately, it is children themselves who must decide the degree they wish to work on their temper. If there is no willingness on their part to work with you to control obnoxious behavior, you will most likely need to speak to a qualified counselor or therapist.

A good therapist can often help motivate a child to work on anger issues. However, if your problem is not with a small child, but with a teenager, the strategies I've outlined here need to be altered. Indeed, the problems of adolescence are unique, so I've given them their own chapter.

CHAPTER SEVEN

ADOLESCENT ANGER: WHERE IS IT COMING FROM?

- When her parents refused to let her go out without finishing her homework, Jennifer pushed back her chair, stuck her fork into the grilled chicken on her plate, and shouted, "No one, especially you, is going to tell me what to do!" She ran out of the room. Everyone could hear her bedroom door slam shut.
- Steve needed to use the phone. He'd just met the girl of his dreams in study hall that day—and if he didn't get to the phone to call her, he'd lose his nerve. But his little sister was on the phone. "C'mon birdbrain, I need the phone." But she ignored him. Finally, exasperated, Steve grabbed the phone and hung it up. "I told you to get off!" he shouted. His sister went screaming down the hall, looking for her mother.
- Mary always wanted blonde hair instead of what she considered her dirty brown mop. But her mother always told her how pretty and shiny her hair was, that not everyone was born blonde. Mary, a typical teen, didn't put much stock in her mother's opinion. Instead, she went to the drugstore and bought some hair coloring mix. Voila! By the time her mother came home from work, Mary was Madonna blonde. Her mother almost fainted; she screamed. She grounded Mary for a

month and demanded she go with her to a beautician to get her natural color back. Mary couldn't understand why her mother was so angry. *She* was the one who had a right to be furious.

These scenarios are not unusual. It's the age-old conflict between teenager and parent, between independence and dependence, between the push toward adult maturity and the pull of childhood's security.

TO BE A TEEN

The major task of adolescence is achieving independence. Their need to dress a certain way, to be with friends, to rebel against parental values and to test new ones all have the underlying aim of helping them establish their own identities and sense of competence in the world—and eventually to function as mature adults independently from you.

It's important to keep all of this in mind when dealing with adolescents. It helps you remain objective and not take your teen's every contrary stance personally. It also makes it easier for you to understand what is behind much of the anger you encounter in them.

ANALYZING THE ANGER: TEMPEST IN A TEAPOT OR JUSTIFIABLE RAGE?

As I did with younger children in the previous chapters, I'm going to give you a framework to help you analyze your teen's anger. Using their striving for independence as a guidepost, you can determine if the anger is justified— and if it is based on realistic or unrealistic views of the world.

Reality can be an ambiguous term. One way to measure adolescents' ability to be realistic is to see how clearly they understand their responsibilities—work, chores, and school achievements—that they must take care of in order to earn independence.

Here's an example of a "reality check":

John, a 17-year-old, became enraged with his parents when they refused to give him the car keys one evening. He hadn't been keeping up with his chores or schoolwork, and there had been no previous agreement that he could go out. In addition, John's parents themselves had planned to go to a movie. John said his life with friends would be over if he couldn't have the car. He then grabbed the keys from his father's hand and ran out the door.

John's belief that he has the right to the car even though he had done nothing to earn it, reflects both his immaturity and selfishness. His anger is unrealistic—and unjustifiable. In the world at large, people don't get things just because they think they should have them. When an adolescent uses entitlement as a justification for his anger, when he takes an "I want it and I'll take it if I want it" attitude, a major problem exists.

This line of thinking is fundamentally unrealistic—and impractical. In order to preserve such an assumption, the adolescent often resorts to exploiting those around him. Such individuals frequently become bullies, not only to their family, but also to their friends.

If you see this kind of pattern emerging in your adolescent, I strongly recommend seeking counseling before self-defeating attitudes and behaviors become too entrenched, before your teen has serious trouble functioning in his daily life.

I have seen adolescents make unrealistic demands. And when they don't get what they want, they become so angry that they *do* get their desire—through intimidation and fear. This not only alienates them from others, but it also prevents them from realistically assessing their own abilities. Instead, they build up fantasies about themselves which, sooner or later, are destroyed by a clash with reality.

This is a scary situation. But a parent can confront it. You can work to see that your children have a clear understanding of what they have to do to earn certain privileges from the time they are preschoolers. Getting them into the habit of performing chores or tasks to win independence from you instills good work habits. It readies them to function in the real world.

John's anger was undeniably unrealistic. But here's an example of a teen who has every right to be annoyed:

Thirteen-year-old Judy was excited. Her parents promised to take her to a skating outing if she would do three weeks of chores to earn this privilege. Judy complied, but, at the last minute, her parents decided to go to a party to which they'd been invited. They told Judy they would take her skating the next week instead. Consequently, Judy became enraged and rushed into her room—slamming the door and crying.

In this example, Judy did her work to earn her independence. She had every right to expect her reward. But her parents, for whatever reason, denied it to her. They were not consistent. Instead of positive reinforcement, they gave Judy the message that her work was not worth rewarding. They also ran the risk of causing their daughter to lose faith in the value of work—and trust in authority.

No matter what the circumstances, the purpose of analyzing your adolescent's anger, above all else, is to open the door for a dialogue. If teenagers are being unrealistic, for example, your job is to try to correct their misperceptions through discussion and action. And, if they resist your explanations and seem to be developing a skewed view of things, counseling is advisable.

On the other hand, if you learn through your talks that your adolescent is being realistic, you must help him or her make changes in the situation—either by altering things that you do or by helping them to work with others. It is the only way anger will abate.

THE 3 C'S: COPING, CONCEALING, COPYING AND ALL GROWN UP

As with younger children, it is often helpful to try to assess whether your adolescent's anger contains elements of coping, concealing (or protecting), or copying. Because teens have a private life that they don't often share with you, assessing a teen's anger is more challenging than assessing a toddler's rage—but it is not impossible. Testing their realistic versus unrealistic assumptions and determining the "3 C's" can be of considerable value. We've already seen examples of reality versus unreality. Let's now go over the "3 C's" of the teenage years:

COPING

Adolescents sometimes cope with school problems by showing anger. If your son is worried about his grades, for example, he may hide them from you and get angry when you confront him. Adolescents can experience failure in school and drop out. Families may not find out about a teen's school problems until long after they have occurred because of shame and embarrassment. When this is challenged by parents, teens may cope by getting angry.

Anger, as a coping device, can show up at school, at home, and in social situations:

Coping with Poor Performance at School

Fifteen-year-old Stacy recently quit school. When the school social worker asked her why, she said she found the classes boring and that she was tired of having fights with the other kids. She found an 18-year-old boyfriend whom she was visiting regularly, and she enjoyed that much more than being in school. When confronted about the dangers of dropping out of school, she became angry. She screamed and yelled, refusing to talk about the situation any further.

In this case, Stacy chose to avoid doing what young people her age usually do—work in school—because she wasn't performing very well. Instead, she chose what she thought was an easier way through life, i.e., having someone older take care of her. The problem is, of course, that there is a high likelihood that this person will take advantage of her, leading to more problems. By quitting school, she loses her chance to learn valuable skills which she will need if she ever hopes to be independent. Her anger when confronted reflects the insecurity she feels at being incompetent as a student—and the fear that quitting school and leaning on her boyfriend as an alternative is not wise. Her anger is her way of coping with her feelings of helplessness.

Coping with Social Problems

Teens also use anger as a way to cope with problems in their social lives. For example, 15-year-old Richard came home after a party one night and screamed and yelled at his 8-year-old brother to quit making his life difficult. He then became irritable and angry with his parents. It turned out that Richard had broken up with his girlfriend—who had just left him for his best friend. In this case, Richard's anger helps him to cope, albeit in a dysfunctional way, with his feelings of rejection.

Coping with Identity Issues on the Homefront

Forming an identity is a key developmental task of adolescence—which explains why things like hair styles and clothing take on such importance. As many parents know all too well, attempting to persuade teens to alter hair or clothes can arouse fearsome anger, which is often accompanied by protests that to do so would be "disastrous" for their social lives. In this situation, anger is a way adolescents cope with this threat to their identities. It's as though the clothing is a form of armor that protects and defines their fragile sense of themselves. Their adamant defense of their appearance is their way of saying, "This is what I am. It's acceptable to me. And you shouldn't ask questions about it."

"SEEING RED"
Warning Flag

When adolescents use anger as a way of coping with family situations and the family reacts with indifference, it usually means that a serious rift has occurred between the parent and child. When things have gone this far, the adolescent has probably lost faith in his or her parents and, as a result, they may no longer have any influence on his forming identity. In these cases, I would say that counseling is almost always necessary to rebuild the trust necessary for a fruitful parent/adolescent relationship.

Coping with Family Issues

Coping with anger can have many sources in the parent/adolescent relationship. For instance, adolescents often become threatened if their parents scrutinize them too closely. Why? Because they fear exposure of their feelings of inadequacy. For example, Mason, 14, reacts with rage when asked about such minor matters as how he did on a test. In reality, Mason has a lot of doubts about his own abilities in test-taking. His parents' asking him about this undermines his already fragile self-confidence.

Adolescents may also become angry as a way of avoiding getting dragged into conflicts in the family—particularly around such volatile issues as drugs, alcohol, or physical abuse. For instance, Norman's father has a significant drinking problem; he frequently abuses his mother. When Norman came home for dinner one night and his mother announced there would be a family meeting to discuss some problems, he reacted angrily, yelling at his mother and saying, "I'm not going to be around then!" In this case, Norman is using his anger as a smokescreen for his real feelings of fear of getting involved in a possible family conflict, and for his own conflicted pain and deep-seated disappointment at his father.

Concealing, or Protecting

Anger in adolescents can also be a sign that they are hiding something or protecting someone else. When 15-year-old Amy was confronted about staying out of school to be with her boyfriend, she became angry and started a fight. Her anger had been so intense that her parents dropped the subject when she promised to return to school. But, several days later, a similar episode occurred. Her parents soon learned from the school guidance counselor that their daughter had been smoking marijuana when she was at her boyfriend's house. Apparently, she'd use her anger to hide the fact that she was taking drugs.

Sometimes the protecting anger is not a functioning of self-preservation. Sometimes adolescents use anger to protect a special relationship. For example, 13-year-old Skip became extremely angry one night when his parents told him that he couldn't go to a party with his friend. He screamed continuously, saying that it wasn't fair. He refused to discuss the matter further.

It turned out that Skip's friend had told him that their relationship would be over if he didn't accompany him that night. Because he didn't want his parents to know about this relationship and what it meant to him, Skip became angry with them instead. He pretended the issue was unfairness to divert their attention from what really was bothering him.

The use of anger to protect a relationship is particularly common when an adolescent girl becomes involved with an older boy. Parents sometimes notice a drastic, inexplicable change in their daughter's behavior when she becomes involved in this kind of relationship. The same thing can happen with adolescent boys who become part of an older delinquent peer group.

Adolescent anger can also be used to protect family secrets. Teens can get very protective of their families—and show their zeal via anger. They are very sensitive to criticisms about their parents and siblings and they will often react with anger or even violence to conceal the conflicts they may already be feeling themselves about their family problems.

Anger does not exist in a vacuum. Similarly, coping, concealing, and copying may all be present in your child's behavior. Sorting them out and looking at them separately may help you to clarify what is going on.

But anger is not always addressed to an outsider—whether it is a friend or a parent. Sometimes anger can be. . . .

COPYING

In their quest for their own identities, adolescents often use behavior as a way to fit in and be accepted socially by those whom they admire. Thus, they often copy behaviors that they see in others—including anger. Here are examples of how these "Hostile Acts" show themselves:

Hostile Act # 1: Peer Groups

Children who have trouble making friends and have experienced rejection are typically the ones drawn to a hostile group. Worse, they will copy that hostility and make it their own.

George, age 15, is a case in point. In elementary school, he had frequent fights and couldn't seem to make friends. Suddenly, at around age 13, his parents noticed he was hanging around with "different kids." His parents thought this group of youngsters seemed angry; they were worried that he refused to bring them home. To make matters worse, George began staying out to all hours. He started being extremely hostile at home.

The peers in George's group had similar experiences of rejection when they were growing up—and they now avoided dealing with adults. In this kind of peer group, there are usually followers, leaders, and scapegoats. The leader tends to be the person who is the most successful bully. The followers are those who hang around him and who generally respect his wishes. Since the leaders are often angry, younger members often copy this behavior, incorporate it into their personalities, and spill it out when they come home.

One girls' group I know of typifies this phenomenon. Seventeen-year-old Stella had dropped out of school and had become the leader of a group of 15- and 16-year-olds who are always in trouble for truancy. She tells them where they are going to meet, what parties they are going to, and which "tough" guys they'll go out with for a good time. She is known for being fierce and other girls are reluctant to leave the group for fear of her spreading stories about them and assaulting them.

Hostile Act # 2: The Scapegoat

Hostile peer groups almost always include an individual who appears to be the butt of the group, the teen who not only copies the members of the group, but has his own role to play: that of the scapegoat.

Sammy is a prime example. He is 13 and hangs out with

a group of 15- and 16-year-olds who call him names and kick him around. Sammy maintains that he likes hanging around with the "tough guys." Occasionally, they do include him in their plans, and he can't see anything wrong with the situation. He complains that he does not want to be alone and says being picked on is not that bad because he feels accepted by the group.

In looking at the history of someone like Sammy, one often finds that they have played this same scapegoat role in their families. Unfortunately, these "scapegoats" often incorporate the self-blame and loathing into their identity. They often go through life playing the scapegoat role at work, at home, and socially. They often harbor a great deal of unconscious anger for their demeaned rank in life—and they will often express this anger explosively in later life.

If your children have fallen in with a hostile peer group and you are unable to help them extricate themselves, my advice is to seek counseling. These groups are almost always damaging for their members. When children do break away from them and belong to less bullying ones, their anger often dissipates.

Hostile Acts # 3: Learning Anger at Home

As I noted before, children learn a good deal about how to be angry from their home. Two teenage patients of mine, Virginia and John, grew up in a family where their father would frequently come home and browbeat their mother when he had had a bad day. John now has trouble with peers, frequently putting them down. Virginia has trouble standing up for herself. When they are confronted about their difficulties, they both become angry.

They have both learned to react this way from their family. The anger is a part of their identities and has also become a way of coping with fear.

THE INTERNAL ENEMY

Anger turned inward can have many damaging results. Suicide is the end result of this suffocating, unleashed anger and, unfortunately, it is much more common in adolescents than in younger children. Suicide is most likely to occur in impulsive teens and in those suffering from a psychiatric disorder, including depression and substance abuse.

Martha's story is a good example of how depression and anger can lead to a suicide attempt. Martha started withdrawing from her friends. Soon after her boyfriend left her, she began having crying spells. She stayed home from school because she couldn't concentrate and because she felt emotionally paralyzed. Martha's mother also had a history of depression, and that genetic factor made Martha more vulnerable to rejection and loss.

One day, Martha's mother came home from work and discovered that her daughter had overdosed on Tylenol. When she was interviewed by the emergency room doctor, Martha admitted that she was extremely angry because she'd lost her boyfriend. Anger drove Martha's depression and her suicide attempt was evidence that she turned that anger against herself.

John, age 15, is an example of how drug use can fuel anger to such an extent that suicide is attempted. After smoking marijuana and drinking beer one night, he and several of his friends drove down the freeway at 80 miles an hour. They drove off an embankment and ended up in the emergency room. When asked about what happened, John exploded in an angry voice that he didn't care whether he lived or died.

If you notice your child expressing anger in a self-destructive fashion, you should be concerned about an underlying psychiatric disorder. In such instances, a psychiatric and psychological evaluation by a professional is crucial.

* * *

Yes, anger turned inward can be lethal. But it doesn't have to be that way. Nor does anger have to be a self-destructive coping device, a learned behavior, or a way of life. There are constructive, positive ways your teen can deal with anger—which you will soon discover....

CHAPTER EIGHT

HELPING ADOLESCENTS DEAL WITH ANGER

Chris had been a model child, pleasant, helpful, and sweet tempered. But, as she became a teenager, her demeanor changed. She began to wear her hair super-short; she began wearing dark eyeliner; she began wearing three earrings on one earlobe.

At first, her mother tried to ignore the changes. As a single parent, she had enough worries. She assumed that it was just a stage, that her daughter would "come back down to earth."

But things got worse. Soon Chris was staying out late. She had a new group of friends. Her school grades dropped.

It was confrontation time. Unfortunately, Chris and her mother had different agendas. Whenever her mother wanted to broach the subject of Chris's rebellion, her daughter would start ranting and raving. She'd throw things; she'd run up to her room and scream that her mother didn't understand.

Somehow, Chris's mother got her daughter to come see me. When they entered my office, Chris was petulant, defensive, and ready to explode. Her mother was anxious, she smoked too much.

After a thorough evaluation, we began to talk. It turned out that Chris had a learning disability that caused her some problems at school. She'd also been the scapegoat in one of her classes. Apparently, a football hero at her school liked her—which didn't please his current girlfriend too much. This girl, popular and competitive, spread vicious stories about Chris. Consequently, Chris was left out of many things. She became an outcast.

The situation deteriorated. The only group that would accept Chris was a "tough gang." She, in turn, wanted acceptance so much that she took their punk stance—which alienated her even more from her mother and the other kids at school. She also felt guilty; her anger was turning inward. She grasped at the only safe object of her frustrations: her mother. Chris yelled and screamed at her parent in order to conceal her own fears, in order to cope with what she perceived as a very cruel world.

Luckily, they'd come for therapy before Chris's situation grew even more severe. We worked together on various strategies; we discussed Chris's anger, her rejection. She saw a reading specialist to help her with her learning disability. In a few months, Chris had found an equilibrium again. She realized that she had been the unfortunate brunt of someone else's problem. She no longer hated herself. Her schoolwork improved.

And mother and daughter were able to eat dinner together in the evening and laughed.

As with smaller children, your goal with adolescents is to help them control their anger so that it doesn't control them, so that they express it in constructive, emotionally healthy ways. In the same way as with younger kids, teens learn to do this through modeling the behavior they observe in you and other adults. But, because teens are older, you can also teach them by offering constructive suggestions for alternative ways of acting other than exploding in anger.

Since anger in children and adolescents springs from different sources, your approach to angry episodes will vary. Most children accept the fact that their parents have the right to be the bosses in the family. Adolescents, on the other hand, are very likely to question your authority. They also tend to have good vocabularies and arguing skills—which can throw a parent off balance when trying to handle an angry situation.

How do you decide just when your son or daughter has crossed the line from childhood into adolescence so you can know which set of techniques to apply?

At age 11 or 12, children begin to enter adolescence. They experience dramatic growth spurts, their hormones begin to surge, and they take the first steps toward independence. The exact timing of this varies greatly from child to child, but often a child enters a new, more argumentative phase when puberty begins. Although there are no hard and fast rules, the techniques I offer for children work up until the age of 12 or so, while those for adolescence are more practical for those in their teens.

But, for now, it's teen time. And, because adolescents can be more difficult to deal with, it's a good idea to have a specific plan of action when teaching them how to control their anger.

A TEENAGE PLAN FOR ACTION

Anger in adolescents is rarely an isolated occurrence. It's often repetitive, recurring at least once a week. Because of this, you should develop a pattern of responses that you can use in your interaction with your adolescent over a period of time. The three steps I've devised for this purpose cover:

1. Prevention
2. Crisis management
3. Processing

Let's go over each one now:

"Stopping Anger in Its Tracks," or Prevention

Prevention doesn't mean that you'll stop a teenager from ever getting angry. However, you can often help keep an angry outburst from escalating out of control if you're aware of what triggered it—and if you're prepared with a plan of action.

Hal, 16, came home at one am, an hour past his curfew. When his father stopped him in the hallway and tried to confront him about his lateness, Hal became angry and abusive. He stomped off to his room and slammed the door.

Hal's father decided against following his son to discuss the matter. Instead, he thought he would wait until the next morning when both of them would be rested and their anger had subsided. Over breakfast, when they sat down to talk, Hal's father began by saying, "We need to work out a better way of handling these curfews than what happened last night." At that point, his son nodded. He told his dad that he had been late because his friends kept insisting that he wait until they finished listening to some music before he took them home.

Hal and his father then discussed how he might have handled the situation differently. Hal could have called his father and told him he was going to be late. He could have been more assertive with his friends. Hal agreed to do an additional hour's chores at home that week as a repayment to the family for being late.

As this example shows, *the timing of talks is crucial in prevention.* Having your adolescent talk about his objectionable behavior at a time when both of you are no longer angry about the incident is the key to success. The discussion should include what triggered the anger, how your teen dealt with the anger, and how he could have handled things differently. Such a session can be considered successful if both you and your teenager have worked out a way to resolve the conflict.

"SEEING RED"
The Ball Is in Your Court

Even though the techniques for adolescents and children differ, the basic issue is the same: it's up to your children to control their own anger. Your children *must* grasp this issue in order to accept full responsibility for their anger and not try to blame it on you, their friends, the environment, or any other convenient target.

Indeed, as Hal's situation illustrates, fights between teenagers and their family can easily occur because of outside pressure.

But sometimes trying to talk about an angry episode the day after doesn't work. The adolescent can become angry all over again. Consider the following example:

Sue is a 14-year-old who lives with her mother and stepfather. Her mother found $20 missing from her purse one Saturday night after Sue went to a dance. When her mother brought this up with her daughter the following morning, Sue screamed, yelled, and stomped off to her room—refusing to discuss it further.

Unwillingness to deal with an angry episode usually means there's a power struggle going on between the adolescent and her parent. She is, in effect, challenging the parent with a "You-can't-make-me-do-what-I-don't-want-to-do" message. It's almost as if she's forcing her parent into being a jailer.

Under these circumstances, you might try reviewing what the parent/child relationship is all about. Start with a direct question, such as "What do you think the purpose of our relationship is?" If your child falters or comes up with an answer that shows faulty reasoning, you might help her by saying something along these lines: "It's my job to help you learn how to get along in the world so that someday you can function on your own. If I see you doing something that's self-defeating, it's my responsibility to point it out to you and to help you learn more effective ways of living. I want to help you because I love you and want you to be happy. I don't want to be a jailer. I want us to work together."

Sometimes these discussions can open up painful wounds for adolescents. For instance, Julia, a 13-year-old patient of mine, was having a fight with her stepmother about curfews. When her stepmother started talking about her role and how she wanted to help with her future, Julia became tearful and admitted to feeling abandoned by her real mother.

Though it was painful, by exposing Julia's feelings, her stepmother had a better understanding of why Julia was so angry. She also formed a closer bond with her stepdaughter.

But what if your teenager refuses to discuss *any* aspect of an angry episode? If this becomes a pattern, therapy may be necessary for the deadlock to be broken. In these cases, underlying issues usually come out. A problem with authority figures. A pervasive sense of insecurity. A long-standing problem with anger. Whatever the issue, some "time outs" and some therapeutic discussions can be helpful. Because an adolescent possesses some degree of maturity, insight into the fact that he has a temper problem may be enough to motivate him to work on gaining more self control.

"Reaction is Critical," or Crisis Management

What actually constitutes a crisis is often a matter of opinion. For some parents, hearing their teen raise his voice can set them reeling. For others, throwing chairs and punching holes in the wall is tolerated as an acceptable mode of expressing anger. Moreover, individual family members may hold differing views on what a crisis is. This confusion in itself can lead to conflict. Parents may consider it a major crime when their son damages the car, while he might think they are overreacting. One child in a family might think it an affront to be asked to do the dishes before going out on a date, while another will do chores without blinking an eye.

Whatever your definition of a crisis, there are specific ways you can react to your adolescent's anger which may keep it from erupting into a major conflict. Here are the eight strategies I found successful in keeping anger on manageable levels. Because the success of these suggestions depend, in part, on the willingness of your teen to deal with his anger, I encourage everyone to read them. This way, all involved are aware of the ground rules before a potential crisis situation recurs.

To help illustrate these eight suggestions, let's use Violet, age 15, and her mother as an example. Violet was shopping with her mother in the mall and wanted to buy a purple outfit. Her mother felt that the outfit was too revealing and realized that a potential crisis was in the making. To keep things from erupting, she followed these eight rules of thumb:

1. Try to talk to the person when she is alone since audiences inflame anger.

If Violet's mother talked to her in the store with the clerks all around, it's unlikely that Violet would have listened to her. An audience usually serves to get an adolescent's back up. It almost always results in an assertion of independence. Violet's mother wisely told her that they should think more about it; they later discussed the purple outfit when they were sitting alone in the mall having a soda.

2. Always keep on the subject.

In this case, the subject was a particular outfit that Violet's mother thought too revealing. Her reasons for her attitude are what should be discussed. Ideally, she would not allow Violet to divert her attention by talking about other outfits she'd let her buy. She would not dilute her argument with repeated examples of Violet's poor judgment with clothes; this would only provoke Violet and reduce the possibility of a compromise between mother and daughter.

3. Try to preserve your adolescent's self-esteem.

People do not negotiate well when they are attacked and made to feel bad. Noted psychologist Gerald Patterson has pointed out that in order to get someone to change, you may need to give 29 compliments for every criticism. Finding some way to appeal to adolescents' better judgment is always preferable to criticism when trying to get them to see your point of view.

In our example, Violet's mother said, "Honey, I think you know I want you to enjoy your clothes. But in my view it looks silly for a girl your age to wear something so revealing. People will get the wrong idea about you and I don't think you want that. When you're older, if you still want to dress that way, that's your decision. But right now, I don't think it's a good idea."

4. Stick to the present.

Sometimes people dredge up the past as a way of strengthening their position. Perhaps Violet said to her mother, "Remember last time when you didn't let me get what I wanted to wear and you admitted you were wrong?" Her mother would have gotten caught in a trap if she had

---

"SEEING RED"
Time, Place, Person

Angry episodes tend to be repetitive and occur in the same settings. Consequently, in discussions with your teen, it can help you both find the "whys" if you cover:

- **Time.** The particular morning, afternoon, or evening that the incident occurred.
- **Place.** The location where the incident that provoked your adolescent's original anger occurred.
- **Person.** The particular group of people your teen was with at the time.

---

tried to argue this point. Instead, she wisely insisted that they were only going to talk about the purple dress. She also avoided saying such things as, "Remember all the times I bought you whatever clothes you wanted and they stayed in the closet?" Using the past is likely to inflame tempers and accomplishes little except inciting people to dig in their heels.

5. Keep the argument between the two people present.

Insist on using the word "I." People commonly drag others into their arguments by using the word "we"—which only raises the ante. Adolescents often use their "royal we" to make their parent see that they will be ostracized if they don't do what their friends do. Parents resort to the "we" as a way to strengthen their position: "Daddy and I have been around longer than you. We know that these clothes are not becoming to young women."

Using "we" in arguments often has the effect of bringing a sledge hammer to kill a fly. Such tactics usually backfire and alienate parent from teenager.

6. Keep the relationship with the person positive.

When arguing, people sometimes feel they're not being heard and, as a result, attack each other. Violet could have said, "Well, Mother, you don't care how I look, do you? All you care about is yourself." Her mother might have countered: "Well, Violet, if you weren't so selfish and worried about yourself, you might listen to your mom on occasion." These comments move away from the subject, i.e., clothing. They get into the issue of personalities, which only confuse matters.

It also helps to come up with some positive alternative to let adolescents know you want to be helpful and that you're willing to go the extra mile for them. For instance, Violet's mother said, "I'll tell you what, if we don't find something else you really love today, we'll go shopping again later this week and keep looking until we find something smashing." Finding these kinds of solutions may be a challenge to your creativity, but they go a long way towards smoothing ruffled feelings.

7. Stop when you realize you aren't getting anywhere.

Sometimes an adolescent is just not able to hear a parent. When this becomes obvious, there's not much point in continuing.

Generally, you can tell if an argument isn't going anywhere if neither of you has budged after the first two minutes. When Violet's mother realized that her daughter wasn't going to listen to her about the dress, she said, "Well, I see we aren't getting anywhere with this, so let's go home and talk about it later."

After a few hours have passed, emotions and tempers have a chance to cool down; there's a better chance you'll reach some understanding or compromise.

8. Parents and teenagers should *avoid* laying hands on each other.

If one person tries to intimidate another through physical means, productive discussions can never occur. A "time out" needs to be declared between the two parties. Discussion can't be resumed until there's an agreement that intimidation, threats, and the use of force will not be employed by either person in the dispute.

"SEEING RED"
Cool Down

Since the goal is always to cool things down before they boil over, you might agree that if either you or your child raises your voice within 20 seconds of a discussion, you will both take a "time out" for at least five to ten minutes to calm down. It is often helpful to develop a signal which can be used to alert each other that it's time to stop talking and cool down, either blowing a whistle, tapping a pencil, or making the official sports' "time out" sign.

"Thinking It Over," or Processing

As we have already seen, processing anger is an important element in helping someone gain control of his anger. By reviewing exactly what triggered an angry episode, adolescents have a chance to avoid blowing up over the same issue in the future. It also makes them more open to taking some responsibility for the effect their anger has on others.

The success of processing depends, to a large extent, on whether the angry person has any recognition of the problem. Despite the fact that anger has interfered with all areas of his life, a teen can deny he has a problem. If this is the case, specific strategies have to be used to deal with this denial. You might ask your teen to make a note each time his anger gets him into trouble during the day. You might then review these episodes each night. The weight of evidence over a brief time period can convince your teen that a problem exists.

In extreme cases, an adolescent might have several run-ins with the law before he finally deals with his anger. And, of course, there are those unfortunate individuals who never accept responsibility for their anger—and end up paying for it the rest of their lives.

For particularly resistant adolescents, I sometimes recommend they see a school guidance counselor, a juvenile court counselor, or another authority figure who can clarify the legal responsibilities teenagers have to their parents.

RESTITUTION

Any discussion about anger should include mention of its victims. It's very important for angry people to do something to repay those they have injured. The points I'd made about restitution for children can apply to adolescents as well.

For example, if your teens damage property in the house, it's important that they not only fix it, if possible, but also do an additional series of chores. Whatever is chosen, it's important that it means something to the victim. In general, these chores should not take more than about a half hour's worth of work each day—and no longer than three days all told.

During restitution time, the adolescents should also ask the injured person how he felt about the incident. And, at the end of the three days, they should talk with the family about why they did the "payback." This reinforces the message, "If you injure somebody with your anger, you are responsible to pay them back." The point here is not that restitution stops people from being angry—but that *others have feelings just as they do*.

MATURE MINDS MEET

One of the advantages of working with older children is that they can grasp more sophisticated concepts about how anger actually works—physiologically, psychologically, and socially. You can use this newfound intelligence to initiate discussions about how individuals who can't control their anger are really very vulnerable and open to exploitation by others. You can mention how people who use their anger to get what they want usually end up alienating others and getting paid back in the long run. Further, you can talk about some of the anger-reducing strategies we've already discussed, such as the value of trying to calm down before attempting to deal with an explosive issue.

Another advantage of your adolescent's greater maturity is that work on anger problems can be a team effort. This can be especially beneficial if both of you have temper problems.

The best way to approach such a collaboration is to sit down and plan together what you should both do the next time a conflict occurs. You might even find it helpful to draw up a written contract so you can clearly see what expectations you have of each other. Review the strategies for defusing a crisis and incorporate these into your plans.

WITH A LITTLE HELP FROM MY FRIENDS

Practice makes perfect and that's as true with anger control as with any other skill. Consequently, it can only help your teen if he applies everything he learns about anger from you to situations with siblings and friends.

Here's an example. Let's say one of your children is always complaining about being picked on by his older sibling. This older child, in turn, is always being punished by you for his actions. Instead of rescuing the younger child, help the kids figure out how long they usually play together before they start fighting. You can then instruct them how to take "time outs" before a fight begins. In other words, you can help them work together to stop the "angry" problem—and to learn something in the process.

Sibling tensions can build especially when there's a large age gap. It's tempting for the older to bully the younger. As a result, the younger child learns "get even" techniques, such as tattling—which creates even more resentment. Break this cycle by having them draw up a contract to get along better. This contract might include:

- Both children agreeing not to hit each other.
- Both agreeing to take a time out if either requests it.
- The younger child agreeing to tell the older sibling of his complaint *first* before telling the parent, to see if the issue can be resolved without parental intervention.

These techniques can easily be transferred from siblings to friends—when a parent gives practical social advice it strengthens the parent/teen relationship. For instance, Sylvia, age 16, fought regularly with her mother about her new boyfriend. After a year, she also began fighting with her "no longer new" boyfriend. But, since her mother had worked with her on "time out" techniques, she was able to apply these in her relationship with him. They agreed that he should leave her alone a while when she started getting angry.

The success of this strategy also helped Sylvia to be more open with her mother. She listened and agreed with her mother's suggestion that she cut down on intimidating remarks that not only seemed to be getting her into trouble with her boyfriend, but with her other friends as well.

Everyone was pleased with the changes Sylvia made.

STRESS: ANGER'S ENEMY NUMBER ONE

These strategies don't always work. Unfortunately, the techniques I've discussed throughout this book have limitations. Individuals can successfully use them at various points in their lives only to find that, under certain circumstances, all their best efforts to control their anger fail.

This is especially true with teens. Despite an appearance of strength, they are really very brittle, very vulnerable—with a limited tolerance for stress. Teens usually need to reduce the stresses in their lives to prevent anger from becoming a habitual way of coping with problems.

In Alcoholics Anonymous, the stresses, or triggers, that push people into relapse are identified as:

- Hunger
- Anger
- Loneliness
- Fatigue

These are the same triggers that set off temper problems in vulnerable individuals. Helping teens acknowledge, cope with, and manage these "hot spots" will help insure the success of your own Anger Plan of Action.

ANGER BY ANY OTHER NAME

The techniques I've outlined work well with explosive anger. But seething, smoldering, constant anger needs a different approach. So do situations that involve trauma and chronic pain. Let's briefly look at these special situations:

When Revenge is a Factor

Persistent revenge-seeking usually has chronic anger at its root. For example, 13-year-old Alfonse was put in special classes in school because he was always getting into trouble. He'd shoot rubber bands at other children, throw spitballs, or make alienating remarks to the teacher. In fact, he seemed to be in a constant whirlwind of disagreements. But, when he was confronted, Alfonse's response was that other people started it and he had to finish it.

People like Alfonse often find themselves doing battle with everyone and rarely have any friends. They have a chronic need for revenge. This desire to "get even" is often the tip of an iceberg made up of extreme and pervasive discontent. It may also be an indication of depression and self-hatred. The teen may also have been the victim of physical or sexual abuse. In these instances, therapeutic evaluation is recommended.

Chronic revenge-seeking may also be an indication that an individual feels threatened by both intimacy and the fear of abandonment. Helen, a 14-year-old, is a case in point. When she sensed that her new boyfriend might be going out with someone else, she got his best friend to take her out to the mall to arouse her beau's jealousy. The two boys had a fight and, when Helen was confronted about it, she defended herself by saying, "I didn't do anything. I was just paying him back."

In situations like this, revenge is used as a method to control others. Unfortunately, logical explanations don't always help. Telling a teen "if she needs to control her boyfriend, their relationship won't last" usually does no good. It's often necessary for adolescents who behave this way to learn by repeated failures in different relationships that these "holding on" tactics are futile.

Sexual Aggression

Situations where sexuality is mixed with aggression can be particularly troublesome. A 16-year-old patient of mine named Shawn was continually yelling and throwing things at his 11-year-old stepsister—even after he'd been punished for his behavior. One day, he walked in on her in the bathroom. When confronted by his mother, the boy said it was an accident. The next week, he made sexual remarks about her in front of his friends. But, when confronted once again, he claimed it was only a joke.

Things got worse. One night, Shawn awakened his step-sister by looking at her and touching her. A few weeks later, she noticed some of her underwear was missing— which turned up in Shawn's laundry. He denied both incidents.

Jonathan Ross, a well-known expert in this field, has stated that the above incidents are often seen in individuals who eventually become sex offenders. Along with the use of pornography, obscene phone calls, and voyeurism, they are preludes to more aggressive sexual behavior and assault. They often begin in the preteen years or early adolescence.

When deciding if an adolescent is engaging in sexually aggressive behavior, only two things need to be determined:

1. If the offender has power over the victim and...
2. ...if the victim is afraid of being harmed if he or she tells anyone what has been going on.

If there's even a hint of this kind of behavior with your teen, I strongly suggest that you seek help. Often a local mental health center can make an appropriate referral.

Suicidal and Self-Destructive Behavior

You should be aware that people who have made suicide attempts often insist that they are no longer feeling suicidal and that they would never hurt themselves again. But, if they don't understand the triggers that prompted their behavior, these promises don't hold much weight. Since most people have trouble analyzing what drives them to such extreme acts, you should assume that if adolescents express themselves through suicidal behavior once, they might do it again. They need immediate psychiatric evaluation and help.

The same advice holds true for those teens who belittle themselves in order to deal with stress. Therapy with a trained counselor is usually the only way they can learn to express their anger in an appropriate, nondestructive manner.

All the approaches in this chapter require energy, time, and persistence from you and your teen. If you view your work on anger together as the equivalent of taking a course in school, you'll have a sense of how much effort is involved. But, as with any wise investment, the long-term payoff is well worth the effort.

No where is the effort more well worth it than when it comes to dealing with substance abuse, anger, and your teen. This is so crucial a topic that it needs a chapter of its own.

CHAPTER NINE

STREET DRUGS, ALCOHOL, AND ANGER

For people with temper problems taking street drugs is like throwing lighted matches into a gasoline can. They can bring out anger and aggression even in those who'd never shown any prior signs.

If you suspect your teen is using or abusing any drugs or alcohol, I recommend that you seek counseling. Chemical dependency is a very complex problem that is difficult to treat because of the users' denial. Many abusers will actually argue with you about the dangers—as they continue to deteriorate mentally and physically. That's why it's especially important that the counselor be fully qualified and have experience in the complexities of chemical dependency evaluation and treatment.

HOW DRUGS AND ANGER INTERACT

Although people often take drugs initially to "mellow out," the ultimate effect is, ironically, often the opposite.

Regina, age 16, shows how this occurs. Regina tended to get easily stressed in relationships, often becoming jealous or vindictive with her friends. One of them suggested that she try marijuana after school. At first, Regina found that she felt less tense around her friends after smoking a joint.

However, when she began to use marijuana on a regular basis, she experienced a host of other problems. She found herself feeling increasingly depressed. Her old friends dropped away and were replaced with new ones who also used drugs. As a result, drugs became the center of these new relationships and she stopped talking about day-to-day events, developmental issues, fears and enthusiasms with her peers—topics that are so important for young people her age.

Soon problems began to emerge in other areas of her life. Her family became concerned that something was amiss when they first noticed her spending less time with them. They became alarmed when they discovered that she had been hiding drugs around the house. Her grades, too, began to suffer. And, when she stopped using drugs for an extended period of time, her temper would return in full force.

The lesson we draw from this situation is that whatever temporary comfort street drugs may provide, they are no antidote for anger. In fact, they often aggravate it.

CLASS ACTIONS

In this chapter, I hope to give you some general understanding of some of the most commonly used street drugs and their influence on anger.

Basically, drugs can be classified according to their intended effects. Using this system, we can say that there are drugs which are used to get high ("uppers", including inhalants), those which are taken to calm down ("downers"), and those which provide unusual experiences, such as visual hallucinations (hallucinogens).

Classifying drugs according to their effects is an imperfect method. Some drugs have more than one property or they can affect an individual in more than one way. Consequently, I have attempted to pick what seems to be the most important features of a particular drug in placing it in one category over another.

UPPERS

"Uppers" are stimulants which intensify the way an individual sees or feels things. Amphetamines (or in street talk, "speed" and "white crosses") and cocaine are among the best known. Amphetamines are used chiefly to provide a sense of euphoria. Cocaine produces an even more intense high, along with a craving for more that makes it intensely addictive.

Stimulants vary in the effects they have on people's anger. There is always a risk of a person becoming more belligerent when using them. There is also a risk of developing psychotic symptoms. After using cocaine, for example, some individuals may become suspicious, highly explosive and angry because they feel people are against them. Once the effects wear off, the anger lingers. The resulting "down," or depression, can lead to more explosive outbursts. In addition, the urge to get more of the drug frequently promotes physical violence. That's one reason why we frequently hear in the news about the violent death of drug dealers.

Inhalants

Inhalants are products that individuals smell for the purpose of getting high. They include gasoline, white-out, airplane glues containing toluene, fingernail polish, and hairspray. They work by stimulating the brain and replacing oxygen in the lungs. Inhalants are very dangerous and can result in suffocation or seizures—even if used only once. Over time, they dissolve the fat within the brain cells. Further, if the compounds being inhaled also contain metal, such as the lead in gasoline, the brain not only dissolves, but the metal deposits in the brain tissue.

Inhalants don't mellow people's anger. In fact, if a person has not passed out using them, he can become highly volatile and explosive during or after their use. In addition, these compounds can make a user highly suspicious. The combination of anger, irritability, and suspiciousness is very dangerous.

Most people do not use inhalants as a preferred drug. But they might use white-out or other volatile compounds if their preferred choice is not readily available. Unfortunately, some young teens who have preexisting impulse and temper problems preferentially use inhalants. This aggravates their behavioral difficulties.

Violence is most likely to occur in those individuals who had an explosive temper before they began using drugs. By taking a stimulant, what little control people have over their irritability greatly diminishes or disappears altogether. In addition, when people are under the influence of drugs, they don't always remember their violent behavior; they have blackouts.

DOWNERS

"Downers" include:

- Sleeping pills, such as Secobarbital
- Narcotics, such as heroin
- Minor tranquilizers, such as Valium and alcohol

Whether a pill or a narcotic injection, a beer or a shot of whiskey, drugs depress people's moods.

The first question that comes to mind regarding downers

"SEEING RED"
Wise Words

There is a saying in the field of chemical dependency that if you don't have a low I.Q. when you start, after abusing inhalants for even a short time, you will certainly end up with one.

---

is this: Why would people want to *lower* their mood? One reason is that people who prefer downers tend to be more stressed and are usually overstimulated by day-to-day living. They use downers to diminish the anxiety and fear that is their constant companion through life.

In addition, downers are often used in combination with stimulants to flatten or mellow the effects of a high. Unfortunately, "mellowing out" a high does not "mellow out" tempers. In fact, downers are much more likely to make users explosive. Why? Because depression itself usually has elements of anger in it—even if it is turned inward. When people who are angry and anxious take downers, their depressed feelings are often accentuated; they often end up feeling angrier than they were originally.

People taking downers not only become aggressive with others, but they are also liable to engage in self-destructive behavior. Suicide is commonly linked to downers because they cause depression and they diminish impulse control. Both of these factors then promote self destructive acts.

Alcohol

Most teenagers I have worked with don't use tranquilizers, sleeping pills, or narcotics as their major drug of abuse. The most widely used downer among teenagers is alcohol.

Despite its widespread social acceptance, alcohol is an insidiously dangerous drug that can do as much—or more—harm than any street drug. As with other downers, alcohol is *poison* for people with temper problems. It ultimately makes their anger worse. Because it both depresses mood and removes inhibitions, alcohol promotes both anger *and* aggression. Drinking alcohol can even produce explosive behavior and depressive feelings in those who didn't start out with an anger problem.

An interesting illustration of alcohol's effects was found in a study that examined the relationship between the type of music played in bars and the amount of actual violence in the bar. The findings showed that there was much more violence in bars where country and western music was played than in those that played rock music. The researchers reasoned that the sad themes of country and western music—marriages breaking up, relationships ending, loss, and so on—may have stirred depressive feelings in people whose impulse controls were already impaired by drinking.

Without exception, if you see that your teenager has started using alcohol—even if it's infrequent—try to stop it. Alcohol is a dangerous drug. Becoming addicted while a teen is especially dangerous and can lead to problems in later life. If you can't convince your adolescent to stay away from alcohol, I strongly recommend that you take him or her to a counselor who has experience in dealing with chemical dependency.

HALLUCINOGENS

Hallucinogens such as LSD, marijuana, "Morning Glory" seeds, Jimsonweed, and PCP alter the way people feel, see, or hear. Although individuals taking these drugs often claim that they are "mellowed out" from them, I have almost always seen the opposite occur. I know of a young man who assaulted policemen while using PCP. I've also heard reports of people jumping through plate glass windows after taking LSD.

The fact that LSD alters the way people see things is what leads users to have "bad trips." Instead of their distorted perceptions being the pleasant psychedelic images as anticipated, they can turn out to be so frightening and so disorganizing that users lose control and endanger themselves and others.

PCP

Phencyclidine, better known as PCP or angel dust, is an animal tranquilizer which promotes explosive and paranoid behavior even in individuals who show no prior psychological problems.

The PCP stimulates extremely intense feelings while removing a person's ability to control them.

Explosiveness, aggressiveness, self-inflicted injuries, and paranoia are immediate effects of PCP. Depression and suicidal feelings can occur later and last for weeks.

Marijuana

Individuals who use marijuana often report that it helps them feel less irritable. While that may be true for some, it's often a temporary calm. Many others find that they become *more* irritable once the drug wears off. This could be partially a result of marijuana's depressant properties.

Further, individuals who have been using marijuana for a long time often experience intense irritability and explosiveness during a period of withdrawal—which can last three to four weeks.

Although today smoking marijuana is almost as common as drinking alcohol, it is still a drug that can interfere with a person's ability to process and cope with the world.

MIXING DRUGS

Many adolescents don't stick with one drug, but rather, mix them with others in dangerous combinations. One of my patients, Vanessa, age 16, went to a party with her friends and had several beers. She then swallowed a handful of pills that someone offered her with a glass of bourbon. When she passed out and her friends tried to take her home, she became belligerent and started hitting them. She ran out into the street and attempted to take off her clothes.

Taking multiple drugs can drastically decrease the amount of control and awareness people have over their behavior. And, at the same time, it can increase the risk of injury to oneself and to others. It's an explosive combination.

As you can see, street drugs and anger are a volatile mix—and should be avoided. But there are times when prescription drugs can change lives, when medicine can be a useful adjunct in managing anger—as we shall see in the next chapter.

CHAPTER TEN

CAN ANGER BE MEDICATED?

Primum non nocere.

"First, do no harm" is a basic tenet of medicine. When it comes to treating anger with drugs, following this dictum is essential. That's because *all* medications have potentially harmful side effects. Consequently, I only use them when behavioral techniques have proved inadequate—and, even then, only after considering each individual's needs carefully and weighing the risk of side effects versus the potential benefits of the medication.

ANGER MEDICINE

Just how do drugs work on anger? They work in different ways. The types of drugs used to manage anger can be classified according to the actions they have on the body:

1. Medications that decrease irritability, misperceptions, depression, and anxiety—which could all promote anger.
2. Medications that increase attention span and thought organization—thereby making it easier for individuals to cope with the stresses that induce anger.
3. Medications that actually decrease messages of anxiety and fear communicated to the brain and which, as a result, help a person feel more relaxed and less likely to get angry.

WHEN ANGER TECHNIQUES AREN'T ENOUGH

Before you can determine which type of drug is appropriate, you must first determine if medicine is warranted. The following two cases illustrate this need:

Elisha is a 15-year-old who suffered a serious head injury after falling off her skateboard. Several months after the injury, she became irritable and explosive. Her friends and family thought her personality had changed completely. Attempts at "time outs," stress management, and processing were largely ineffective because Elisha acted so impulsively and often without warning.

John is a 17-year-old who had been very irritable and explosive for many years. He had fights with other kids in practically all of his classes. Now he is fighting regularly with his girlfriend; he is breaking and smashing things at home. In one fit of rage, he knocked his father out. Behavioral strategies, such as counting to ten, have helped somewhat to decrease the number of these episodes, but their intensity continues to remain the same.

These are only two scenarios in which pharmacotherapy might be useful. Other cases include those in which an individual has a specific psychiatric or medical condition, such as temporal lobe epilepsy, manic-depressive disease, intermittent explosive disorder, attention deficit hyperactivity disorder, Tourette's syndrome, obsessive-compulsive disorder, panic disorder and phobias, depression, psychosis, and sleep disorders. (See Chapter Four for more details on these disorders.)

EFFECTS OF DRUGS
FOR AGGRESSION MANAGEMENT

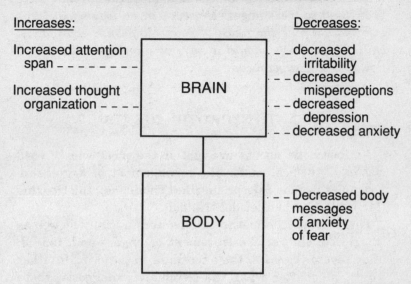

Increases: Decreases:

Increased attention   _ _ decreased
  span _ _ _ _ _ _ _ _   irritability
                                              _ _ decreased
Increased thought   BRAIN   misperceptions
  organization _ _ _ _   _ _ decreased
                                                    depression
                                              _ _ decreased anxiety

                         BODY   _ _ Decreased body
                                                    messages
                                                    of anxiety
                                                    of fear

But drugs are not a panacea. For them to be effective, the children or teenagers for whom they are prescribed must be agreeable to using them. If they are not, studies have shown that they'll find some way to avoid taking them. Because of this, I always explain why I think the medication is necessary and why it will be helpful. I also allow patients the option of refusing it. I believe it's everyone's right to decide what goes into his body.

Further, before medication is prescribed, behavioral and psychological assessment followed by psychological treatment should be tried. Medication should never replace psychotherapy. I can not think of any instance in which medication should be given *without* being accompanied by psychological treatment. The medication can treat the anger directly, but the therapy can treat the underlying environmental problems that cause and sustain the anger. Medication can be a part, albeit an important one, of a comprehensive approach to helping children and adolescents tame the brittle giant within.

To help guide you through the medication maze, I've included some descriptions of the medications that have been used to treat anger. *However, in no way should this information take the place of counseling with your physician. These drugs should always be administered under a doctor's close supervision.*

ANTIPSYCHOTIC AGENTS

Antipsychotic agents are one of the most widely used classes of medication for the management of aggression. Examples include chlorpromazine (Thorazine), thioridazine (Mellaril), and haloperidol (Haldol).

These antipsychotic medications were initially viewed as "magic bullets" for the treatment of anger—and, indeed, after several decades, they continue to perform. In other words, no matter what the psychiatric diagnosis, these medications could be relied on to sedate. Whether antipsychotics suppress anger by decreasing it physiologically, by decreasing the distorted thinking that leads to anger, by simply sedating an individual—or a combination of all three—is not entirely clear. However, they are double-edged swords and have to be administered with great care. They are no longer considered "magic."

Here's an example to show you why: Nine-year-old Mike was very aggressive; he hit and kicked others, smashed toys and had hour-long tantrums. Psychiatric examination revealed that he had had trouble controlling his temper for some time and that, when he got angry, he felt everyone was against him. A trial of Mellaril, 50 mg. a day, produced a marked decrease in his tantrums for several days. However, Mike became quite sleepy within a half-hour to an hour after each dose and he had trouble concentrating.

After Mike had been on this medication for several weeks, it no longer seemed to be as effective and the dose had to be increased. In addition, every week or two, Mike would gain a pound—despite his efforts to limit his food intake.

As this case shows, there are both benefits and side-effects of antipsychotic medication. They are not a cure-all for aggression—but they can be useful in a crisis. One problem with regulating antipsychotics is that even though angry outbursts are repetitive, they can occur hours or even days apart. If someone is put on a daily dose of antipsychotic medication, he may be medicated even when he doesn't need to be.

On the other hand, using antipsychotic medications on an "as needed" basis often doesn't work as well because most of these drugs take between 45 minutes and an hour-and-a-half to become effective. By that time, many children and adolescents have already begun to calm down. In addition, there's a risk of developing potentially permanent facial tics (Tardive Dyskinesia) with long-term use.

For all these reasons there has recently been a trend away from using antipsychotic medications as a treatment for anger. In fact, in a draft of its "parameters of care" on the treatment of conduct disorders, The American Academy of Child Psychiatry strongly discourages the use of antipsychotic medication in the management of conduct disorders.

Although I have emphasized the risks of antipsychotic medication use, I can remember individuals for whom these drugs have been beneficial.

In general, individuals who have a positive response to antipsychotic medications are those who show distorted thinking patterns and may have a history of schizophrenia in the family. For example:

• Juanita, 9-years-old, had frequent temper tantrums and did not follow rules in school or at home. One day she set fire to her brother's bed because she was angry with him. On another occasion, she threw another student's lunchbox out the school bus window because he called her friend a name. She showed no understanding of her behavior. After taking

Stelazine—1 mg. per day for a week—her behavior became more organized and less aggressive.

- Seven-year-old Anthony, would get angry and hit his father and his teacher when assigned homework or chores. Although these behaviors only occurred once or twice a week, when they occurred they disrupted the class and the family. Anthony's tantrums were violent and he appeared unable to stop them. When he took Haldol—1 mg. per day—he had increased ability to understand his behavior and cooperate with family and school rules. Although he continued to become angered, he had better control over tantrums and assaults.

- Judy, 8-years-old, was frequently irritable and had many screaming fits when requested to do chores or schoolwork. She had few friends, because she destroyed their toys and fought with them. She spent a lot of time by herself, and told her mother that she heard her grandmother's voice telling her "bad" things. Her grandmother had lived with the family for several years before moving away after a fight with Judy's mother. The grandmother had once been hospitalized for a schizophrenic psychosis. When treated with 30 mg. of Mellaril, Judy spent less time alone and was able to play with a friend for an afternoon without fighting. After a month of taking Mellaril, Judy reported that she no longer heard her grandmother's voice.

ANTICONVULSANTS

Fifteen-year-old George was known for his bad temper. He had been suspended three times during the school year for starting fights in class. At home, he became upset over extremely minor confrontations; he frequently punched holes in the wall. In the course of the evaluation of his problem, George was kept awake for 24 hours and then given an electroencephalogram to record his brain wave patterns. The test revealed that he had abnormal electrical discharges in his temporal lobes—which was diagnosed as temporal lobe epilepsy, the most common type of epilepsy associated with angry outbursts.

George's anger responded to Tegretol, which has been beneficial for many people suffering from temporal lobe seizures. It is not clear whether Tegretol reduces anger because it reduces the seizures or if it's effective because it increases impulse control.

Whichever it is, Tegretol often works. A person with temporal lobe epilepsy taking this medication may, like George, feel less angry when faced with limits, provocative remarks, and tense situations.

However, Tegretol is not without side effects. Because it lowers white blood cell count and can, on occasion, increase liver enzymes, it's important to monitor both blood and liver function levels. And, because Tegretol's effectiveness depends, as with most medications, on a person having a therapeutic blood level in his system, this too should be monitored carefully.

But George's epilepsy illustrates only one type of seizure disorder. Other seizure disorders include those in which individuals show uncontrollable body movements and become unconscious, those in which they have staring spells, and those in which they have selective movements of part of their bodies.

In these cases, abnormal electrical discharges in areas of the brain other than the temporal lobes may be associated with irritability and temper outbursts. Depakote (Valproic Acid) may be effective in controlling anger in some of these disorders. But, here, too, there are side effects: weight gain and (rarely) liver toxicity. Liver chemistry should be carefully monitored as well as blood levels for safety and efficacy.

Sometimes, however, an anticonvulsant doesn't work. That's when Propranolol, a beta-blocker and blood pressure medication, may be useful. Studies have seen dramatic results in some brain-damaged individuals who take Propranolol. Their aggressive behavior decreased from an almost constant condition to a rare occurrence.

Propranolol has also been effective in instances where individuals have a history of explosive behavior combined with learning disabilities, and/or attention deficit hyper-activity disorder.

Its chief side-effects are sleepiness, depression, lowered pulse rate, and lowered blood pressure. The optimum length of time an individual should stay on Propranolol is not known. Thus, reducing it after a few months to see if the anger remains controlled may be advisable.

ANTIDEPRESSANTS

Anger is not always caused by seizure or psychosis. As we have seen in Chapter Four, anger can be a symptom of depression—especially in the smoldering, self-defeating re-venge type of anger. In cases where the depression is severe and suicide is a possibility, an antidepressant medication is sometimes administered, *always* along with psychotherapy.

There are a variety of antidepressant medications avail-able to treat depression, and its anger symptoms. Among them are:

- **Imipramine** (Tofranil) This is the most widely used antide-pressant for children and adolescents.
- **Desipramine** (Norpramin)
- **Amitriptyline** (Elavil)
- **Nortriptyline** (Pamelor)
- **Fluoxetine** (Prozac) A newer antidepressant, this has had promising results among young people.

If an antidepressant medication is prescribed, monitoring is essential. A physical exam, cardiogram, pulse rate and blood pressure readings should be performed on a regular basis. Further, blood levels should be monitored to prevent drug toxicity and to insure that the medication is at thera-peutic levels—especially when imipramine, desipramine, or nortriptyline is prescribed.

Results from antidepressants may take as long as four to six weeks to be seen. Their side-effects can include weight gain, nausea, dry mouth, fatigue, and constipation—although these are often temporary. In a few cases, Prozac has been associated with self-destructive behavior in adults. Although most of the children and adolescents I have worked with have tolerated it well, if anyone shows signs of becoming explosive or irritable while on Prozac it should be discontinued. There have also been three reports of sudden death with desipramine, although the circumstances leading to these are unclear. Overall, these are very useful medications.

Antidepressants have consistently helped thousands of people since they have become available.

LITHIUM

When depression is combined with manic episodes, anger can take on an explosive air. For manic-depressive illness, the medicine of choice is a natural sea salt called lithium.

Although individuals with manic-depressive illness usually need to be on lithium for extended periods, it's unclear how long people who have anger problems need to take it.

But, whether short-term or long, people on lithium need to have their blood levels closely monitored to make sure they are getting the right amount.

Some of its side effects include fine tremors, excessive drinking, frequent urination, hypothyroidism, and weight gain. Excess amounts can cause confusion and even death.

THE FUTURE IS NOW

There are several areas of investigation that may alter our treatment approach to aggressive children and teenagers, such as advances in PET—or Positron Emission Scan-

Medicines for Aggression Management

Medicine Class Medicine Example	Intended Purpose	State of Knowledge	Possible Side-Effects/Risk
Antidepressant Imipramine	• Antidepressant • Increase attention span	Many journal articles	Depends on drug; some, weight gain, rapid pulse, elevated blood pressure; others, irritability. Many side effects controlled by dose
Antipanic	• Decrease underlying panic disorder	Many studies in adults	Same as antidepressants
Antiobsessive	• Decrease underlying obsessive-thoughts	Many studies Treatment of obsessive-compulsive disorder	Depends on drug. Some irritability, some same as antidepressants
Centrally acting hypertensive agent/Catapres	• Decrease underlying Tourette's or attention deficit disorder	Several studies—Use increasing in trials over last five years	Fatigue, low blood pressure, dry mouth
Benzodiazepine/Ativan	• Decrease underlying anxiety • Decrease sleepwalking • Decrease night terrors	Most studies with adults	Can be addicting; get opposite effect-agitation instead of sedation. "Hangover" with long acting benzodiazepine, depression

Antipsychotic/Mellaril	• Decrease agitation • Improve ability to think clearly	Use is common	- Weight gain - Failure to be effective and need to increase dose - Irreversible movements from long term use
AntiEpileptics/Tegretol	• Decrease seizure activity • Decrease rages	Use with epilepsy-Common Use with rage attacks-New	- Depends on drug. - May include low WBC count, liver enzyme elevation, weight gain
Beta Blockers/Propranolol	• Decrease rage attacks	Experimental	Few, if monitored, and dose controlled - low pulse, low blood pressure, depression
Lithium Carbonate	• Stabilize mood • Decrease irritability	Used more frequently in last decade with children for aggression control and manic/depressive symptoms	Thyroid, kidney functions and lithium levels need monitoring - tremors, frequent urination, excess drinking water, nausea, weight gain may occur

• *Not all inclusive. Consult PDR*

ning, research about the role of serotonin in the brain, and work with the body's endorphin system which generates the body's own "pain medication." As of June 1991, research in these three areas is preliminary, but it holds exciting possibilities for the future:

Brain Activity and Positron Emissions Scans (PET Scans)

A recent *New England Journal of Medicine* report suggests that some hyperactive kids may use glucose differently in some parts of their brain than other children. These results came from studies which used PET scans—diagnostic "X-rays" that actually show brain activity as it happens— via computerized photographs of specially labeled glucose, swallowed by the patient, as it courses through the brain. Over the next few years, PET scans will likely become so sophisticated that it will be possible to see not only where glucose is metabolized in the brain, but where other chemicals, such as mood-influencing Norepinephrine and Serotonin, are metabolized. It may even be possible to compare the differences in metabolism between people with explosive anger and revenge-type anger—which may help in future diagnosis and treatment.

Increased Interest in the Neurochemical Serotonin

Low serotonin levels in spinal fluid has been associated with both increased suicide risk and with being impulsive. Blood serotonin levels are also being looked at as reported in *Audio-Digest Psychiatry* (a twice-monthly audio cassette psychiatric update for physicians from the California Medical Association) to see if they are also a marker for aggressive behavior. If the work turns out to be clinically important, it's possible that chemicals which raise serotonin levels may help certain individuals control their anger more satisfactorily.

Advances in the Body's Own
"Pain Medicine"—Endorphins

Research with autistic and retarded children has found some interesting results with drugs that stimulate the body's own "pain medicine"—the endorphin system. Drugs, such as naloxone or naltrexene, have been used in some preliminary studies to see if they decrease the self-destructive behavior usually associated with autistic and retarded children—such as biting themselves, banging their heads, and other forms of angry self-mutilation. Results of these drug tests are not yet conclusive, but they may have exciting implications for people suffering from self-destructive behavior.

"SEEING RED"
Truth Is In The Stopping

In order to find out if a medication is truly beneficial, I often recommend stopping it for a while—even if the person is responding favorably. This way I can see if it's the medication that's causing the improvement or whether it's some change in the environment.

CHAPTER ELEVEN

WHEN THERAPY IS CALLED FOR

Yes, anger *is* a normal emotion. But when anger gets out of control, when it starts to rule and ruin an individual's life, it becomes almost an illness in and of itself. Like a flailing giant, unhealthy anger can be as destructive a force in a person as any serious mental disturbance. But, in most cases, catching the problem before it gets too extreme can prevent your child or adolescent from much unhappiness and trouble in later life.

KNOWLEDGE IS POWER

Although the approaches I've presented throughout this book should help you assist your child in dealing with anger in most situations, sometimes outside intervention is necessary. And that's where therapy may help.

When all else has failed, when the problem is too big or

gone too far for you to handle, or when you feel uncertain and overwhelmed, it can be the only option. Professional help can take the form of medication (as we have seen in the previous chapter), but always in conjunction with other types of therapy.

WHAT KIND OF THERAPY IS RIGHT FOR YOU? TALKING IT OUT

There are many different types of therapy and many different approaches. All of them can work in treating anger. But, in order for any therapy to be successful, a person must:

1. Realize that his anger is fundamentally his own problem. If he does not choose to control it, no one else is going to be able to do it for him.
2. Come to see that using anger to manipulate or intimidate is socially and personally destructive—even though it may produce temporary, short-term gains.
3. Embark on a therapy that not only focuses on the need to deal with anger, but the need to perform restitution for the victim as well. As we have seen, anger affects not only the individual but victims as well. Holding the aggressor accountable for property damage and/or injury to others is critical if therapy is to have an impact.

OUTCASTS

Therapy usually takes place on an outpatient basis, once or several times a week. The amount of time outpatient treatment needs to be successful varies considerably from individual to individual. If, for example, I'm treating a child who's had an anger problem for several years, I like to see him or her for three to six months. At that time, I'll review our sessions to help the child and family assess what progress has been made and what goals should be set for future treatment—if needed.

A main ingredient in successful, short-term therapy is trust. But sometimes it's extremely difficult to develop a trusting, comfortable relationship with a patient. Without trust, patients might not hear what I'm saying. They might hesitate doing anything I suggest. They might not see that what I suggest may be of help to them.

"SEEING RED"
Trust Is a Must

The position I take in working with angry teens is that I can be of help *only* if they want me to be. I take the same position with families as well. I point out that if teens do not want to control anger, it will never happen. This position not only helps teens develop a sense of control over themselves, but it also encourages the family to hold teens more accountable for their actions—which will stop bad angry "habits" from being reinforced.

In those cases where trust is absent, therapy takes longer. It can take several years to establish an alliance. Sometimes one fails, and no alliance or treatment occurs.

THE BASIC "FOOD FOR THOUGHT" GROUPS

There are three basic "food for thought" groups of therapy, three therapeutic forms that have had success in treating anger, either separately or in concert with each other. They are family, individual, and group therapy. Let's briefly review them now:

It's All in the...Family Therapy

Here, the individual is viewed and treated in the context of the larger family system. Anger and other unhealthy

---

"SEEING RED"
Therapy Recipe # 1: Mood Disorders

Individuals who are depressed and angry require a two-pronged approach to therapy. Both the underlying elements that caused the depression (e.g., low self-esteem, hopelessness, and helplessness) and the anger itself must be addressed if the treatment is to be beneficial.

---

behavior is seen as a symptom of family dysfunction. For example, marital problems, one parent or sibling with a psychological or physical illness, financial woes, or more subtle, perhaps unspoken, family conflicts are often discovered to be in some way promoting the child's or adolescent's anger.

The main tenet in family therapy is that if the family's problems are improved, the child's symptomatic behavior will decrease. By treating the whole family, the therapist gets an added advantage: He or she has the opportunity to observe the counterproductive ways parents might be dealing with their child's anger. The therapist can then offer more effective solutions.

Some of the "utensils" used in family therapy include:
• **Genograms.**
These have nothing to do with the family jewels. They are, like those done for the queens and kings of England, family history charts or trees which enable a child to connect his aggressive behavior to the behavior of other relatives from earlier generations. Family similarities can promote understanding and a degree of relief to the angry child.
• **Contracts.**
Negotiating and signing a contract works. When it is

done within the context of family therapy, discussions of past episodes give the family members the opportunity to share secrets, to "open up" and reveal old pain, old truth. And, when the actual contract is written, step-by-step plans for the future can be included to stop undesirable behavior.

These contracts between parent and child can contain specific ways a child can deal with anger and the consequences of failing to live up to the agreed-upon terms. It can give parents the opportunity to show their understanding and appreciation of their child's needs.

It's Up to the... Individual Therapy

It's exactly as it sounds: one-on-one, concentrated and focused. In individual therapy, children or adolescents have the opportunity to discuss *in detail* those issues in their lives that are bothering them. When anger is one of those issues, a competent therapist will try to get children to see how they use it as a way to protect their feelings when threatened. The therapist will help children realize how anger can promote retaliation which is out of proportion to the initial hurt.

Through successful individual therapy, patients will come to realize that, despite its short-term gains, anger usually results in long-term liabilities—such as alienation from family and friends, loss of education opportunities and job advancement, the break-up of important and meaningful relationships.

Some of the "utensils" individual therapy uses are:

• **Learning Triggers.**

Early on in individual treatment, children or adolescents should be able to see that their anger is usually set off by the same events—and that, as a result, their outbursts can be predicted and planned for before they happen. They can

---

"SEEING RED"
Therapy Recipe # 2:
Seething, Revengeful Anger

People with this type of smoldering anger have to be convinced that the positive aspects of relationships are more important than the feelings of triumph they experience when getting revenge over someone who has done them wrong. In treating people with revenge anger, I've sometimes found that low self-esteem is at the root of the need to put others down. Getting to this underlying cause is often a significant first step in helping them to break out of self-defeating behavior patterns.

Cognitive therapy is a short-term behavior therapy that deals with the negative thoughts and beliefs that provoke people into erroneous, self-destructive action. It has been found to enhance a depressed person's self-esteem while providing specific anger control strategies.

---

begin to understand what underlying issues may be provoking their anger.

Harboring some kind of secret. Low self-esteem. Self-hatred. Social or academic failure. All these can be at the root of problem anger, all these can "trigger" an angry outburst—and can be prevented with understanding and a solid plan.

• **Getting to the Bottom of Revenge.**

The benefits children with revenge problems reap in individual therapy comes from reviewing and analyzing the way they perceive the world. Often, it turns out that revenge-style behavior develops from a feelings of a lack of control over one's environment. Revenge "battles" give the

perpetrator an illusion of control because other people are
forced to deal with him.

On the other hand, if children or adolescents react to
something with explosive, intense rage, I have found that
usually means an event or situation has special meaning
for them. For instance, a young patient of mine responded
in a furious rage when his friend stuck his finger in his
back and said, "I'm going to shoot you."

It turned out that this boy had been molested at gun-
point two years earlier—which dramatically illustrates the
therapeutic importance of understanding the source of an
individual's anger.

There's Safety in ... Group Therapy

In group therapy, individuals have the opportunity to
talk about themselves as well as to learn from others with
similar problems. For many, it is the first time they have
had a chance to compare notes with peers about such
pertinent issues as self-esteem, family problems, rejection,
and school failure. The support and understanding they
receive is usually very beneficial.

WHEN HOSPITALIZATION BECOMES AN OPTION

A trial of outpatient therapy almost always precedes
inpatient or residential treatment. Often, however, a family tolerates a child's or adolescent's explosive behavior for
years—until one incident becomes the proverbial last straw.

Take the case of 16-year-old Ralph. He had been bullying
his family into getting his own way for years. He was even
able to manipulate his parents into letting him quit school
by promising he'd get a job.

Indeed, his family was completely defeated—to the point
where his parents even let him have the family car to keep
the peace. One day, however, Ralph's father decided to

stand up to his son. He refused to hand over the car keys. Ralph struck his father. A fist fight ensued. Ralph tried to get the car keys by threatening to break the windshield if he didn't get them. Ralph won. But, when he drove off, his father called the police. He felt he could no longer manage his son.

At the orientation interview to the adolescent program at the hospital, Ralph's parents said that he had been terrorizing them for years. They had suggested therapy, but he'd been unwilling to go. They now felt that hospitalization was the only recourse.

Impulsive individuals such as Ralph are often poorly motivated to get better—which is why outpatient therapy rarely works for them. Typically, however, children or adolescents have been through some kind of outpatient therapy for some time before parents decide on hospitalization. It is the choice of last resort.

WHY HOSPITALIZATION?

The one main benefit of inpatient treatment: it provides a contained environment where children can be observed and supervised 24 hours a day. This enables the therapist to set limits on children's behavior, to hold them accountable, and to require that they perform restitution for any aggressive acts. As a result, children can practice understanding and coping with anger and with those situations that provoke it, in a safe, structured environment.

A JOURNEY OF A 1000 MILES BEGINS WITH THE FIRST STEP

One of the first steps in an inpatient setting is a thorough evaluation to determine if there is a possible medical cause for the anger, such as temporal lobe epilepsy or manic-depressive illness.

"SEEING RED"
Therapy Recipe # 3:
Juvenile Manic-Depressive Disease

This disorder is often difficult to diagnose because it looks somewhat like hyperactivity disorder or a behavior disorder. Therapy for these children should aim at stabilizing mood through medication, individual therapy, and anger management.

Therapy Recipe # 4: Psychotic Disorders

These disorders are often significantly improved with medication. Therapy should focus on ways individuals can function more realistically in their environment while, at the same time, cope better with anger. Group therapy is often very helpful.

Next comes the psychological interview. When I talk to adolescents in our program for the first time, I usually ask them what makes them angry, how they show their anger, and how they are going to control it in our facility. I try to help put teens at ease, to offer security and trust.

I then explain, step-by-step, our program for anger control. One of our regulations, for example, is that patients take "time out" when they are angry, either in their rooms or in a special "time out" room—and that they refrain from assaulting others.

I also firmly but compassionately explain how privileges within the hospital setting can be earned for following these rules—which will help reinforce appropriate behavior.

Once the rules and structure of the milieu are tacitly accepted by the child or teen, therapy can begin. Individual therapy can occur as frequently as once a day.

Family and group therapies are also part of the hospital routine. Medication, too, can be carefully monitored and supervised within the hospital setting.

Hospitalization, however, is no panacea. A child or teen who, despite parents, therapists, and staffs best efforts, refuses help will not improve. Children who are biologically vulnerable and unresponsive to medications and therapy also may not get better. Fortunately, in my experience, the number of children who are treatment resistant have been few.

THE FIRST CHALLENGE

Whatever their approach, therapists in inpatient settings often find they have to continuously remind patients that they are not jailers—but teachers. Angry young people often view therapists as "prison guards" because of their tendency to blame others for the problems they themselves have caused.

Indeed, one of the first challenges inpatient therapists and staff have is to try to get young people to view them as guides, teachers, people to be trusted. In this role, therapists have a better chance of being listened to when they offer suggestions and lessons about anger control.

From medication to individual therapy, from group situations to family talks, treatment can work, offering help—and hope—for those with anger disorders.

Anger, by itself, is not destructive. Provoked by valid situations, and handled constructively, anger is a necessary and helpful outlet.

But, as we have seen throughout the pages of this book, anger can be misdirected—explosive, seething, and sometimes out of control. When this happens to your children, the results can be immeasurable pain and frustration—for the entire family.

However, as we have also seen throughout this book,

"SEEING RED"
Therapy Recipe # 5:
Attention Deficit Hyperactivity
Disorders and Learning Disabilities

Learning skills and anger control management should be the focus of therapy for children with these disorders. Some patients with learning disabilities are better able to learn from a printed page while others do better when the information is spoken. These learning differences must be recognized if treatment is to be effective.

Therapy Recipe # 6: Substance Abuse

Abstinence must be the focus of therapy for people whose anger is either exacerbated by or simply expressed with drugs and alcohol use. An Alcoholics Anonymous/ Narcotics Anonymous approach, which stresses the 12-step program, can be very effective with adolescents. I have found an excellent step program workbook developed by Dr. Steven Jaffe which has been very helpful for my patients. The Hazelden program in Minnesota is also an excellent source of information about adolescent chemical dependency.

Therapy Recipe # 7: Sexually Assaultive Behavior

Sexually aggressive behavior requires special treatment. In general, individuals who engage in sexually aggressive behavior often profit from group therapy because potential sex offenders often feel "different" and that no one understands them. Being able to talk with others with similar problems lessens their alienation— which can be a first important step in therapeutic change.

I have also found the psychoeducational curriculum developed by Jonathan Ross for potential sex offenders quite helpful for my patients.

there are strategies that can help you deal with anger problems in your children.

They do take time.
They do take some effort.
But they work.
Anger problems can be understood, managed and controlled.

For the individual and his family, mastery of this problem can enhance individual self-worth and bring about a new, more satisfying closeness within a family.

SOURCES

Besag, Valerie, *Bullies and Victims in Schools: A Guide to Understanding and Management.* New York: Taylor & Francis/Open University Press, 1989.

Brent, David A., "Correlates of the Medical Lethality of Suicide Attempts in Children and Adolescents," *Journal of American Academy of Child Psychiatry* Vol. XXVI (January 1987), pp. 87–89.

Campbell, Magda; Cohen, I.L., and Small, A.D., "Drugs in Aggressive Behavior," *Journal of the American Academy of Child Psychiatry*, 21:2, 107–117 (1982).

Carlson, G.A., and Cantwell, D.P., "Suicidal Behavior and Depression in Children and Adolescents," *Journal of American Academy of Child Psychiatry*, Vol. XXI (July 1982), pp. 36–68.

Casat, C.D.; Pleasants, D.Z., and Fleet, Judith, "A Double-Blind Trial of Bupropion in Children with Attention Deficit Disorder," *Psychopharmacology Bulletin*, v. 23, no. 1, (1987) p. 120–122.

Chess, S., and Chess, Thomas A., *Annual Progress in Child Psychiatry and Development*, vol. 10. New York: Brunner/ Mazel, 1977.

Erikson, Erik H., *Childhood and Society*. New York: W.W. Norton, 1964.

Evans, Randall, W., et al, "Carbemazepine in Pediatric Psychiatry," *Journal of American Academy of Child and Adolescent Psychiatry*, vol. XXVI (January 1987), pp. 2–8.

Gardner, M., *The Deadly Innocents*. New Haven, Conn.: Yale University Press, 1985.

Galdston, Richard, "The Domestic Dimensions of Violence: Child Abuse." *Psychoanalytic Study of the Child*, vol. 36 (1981), pp. 391–414.

Goldstein, Harris, S., "Cognitive Development in Inattentive Hyperactive, and Aggressive Children: Two- to Five-Year Follow-up," *Journal of American Academy of Child Psychiatry*, vol. XXVI (February 1987), pp. 214–18.

Grad, Linda R.; Pelcovitz, David; Olson, Madelyn; Matthews, Michael, and Grad, Gary J., "Obsessive-Compulsive Symptomatology in Children with Tourette's Syndrome," *Journal of American Academy of Child Psychiatry*, vol. XXVI (January, 1987) pp. 69–73.

Gross, Mortimer, D.; Tofanelli, Ruth A.; Butzirus, Sharylk, and Snodgrass, Earl W., "The Effects of Diet's Rich in and Free from Additives on the Behavior of Children with Hyperkinetic and Learning Disorders," *Journal of American Academy of Child Psychiatry*, vol. XXVI (January 1987), pp. 53–55.

Halperin, Jeffrey M., "Relationship Between Stimulant Effect, Electroencephalogram, and Clinical Neurological Findings in Hyperactive Children," *Journal of American Academy of Child Psychiatry*, vol. XXV (June 1986), pp. 820–25.

Handford, H., et al, "Depressive Syndrome in Children Entering a Residential School Subsequent to Parental Death, Divorce, or Separation," *Journal of American Academy of Child Psychiatry*, vol. XXV (March 1986), pp. 409–15.

Hollander, Harriet E., et al, "Characteristics of Incarcerated Delinquents: Relationship between Development Disorders, Environmental and Family Factors, and Patterns of Offense and Recidivism," *Journal of American Academy of Child Psychiatry*, vol. XXIV (January 1985), pp. 221–26.

Hsu, L.G.K., et al, "Is Juvenile Delinquency Related to an Abnormal EEG?" *Journal of American Academy of Child Psychiatry*, vol. XXIV (March 1985), pp. 310–15.

Hunt, R. D., et al, "Clonidine-Benefit Children with Attention Deficit Disorder and Hyperactivity: Report of a Double Blind Placebo-Crossover Therapeutic Trial," *Journal of American Academy of Child Psychiatry*, vol. XXIV (May 1985), pp. 617–30.

Jaffe, Steven, Step Workbook for Adolescent Chemical Dependency Recovery, *American Academy of Child & Adolescent Psychiatry*, 1990.

Jenkins, et al, "Status Offenders," *Journal of American Academy of Child Psychiatry*, vol. XIX (February 1980), pp. 320–34.

Kashiani, J., et al, "Depression and Depressive Symptoms in Preschool Children from the General Population," *Journal of American Academy of Child Psychiatry*, vol. CXLIII, September, 1986, 1138–1144.

Klovin, I; Miller, F.J.W.; Fleeting, M., and Kolvin, P.A., "Social and Parenting Factors Affecting Criminal-Offence Rates: Findings from the Newcastle Thousand Family Study, 1947–1980," *British Journal of Psychiatry*, vol. 152 (1988), pp. 80–90.

Lewis, Dorothy O., et al, "Homicidally Aggressive Young Children: Neuropsychiatric and Experiential Correlates,"

American Journal of Psychiatry, CXL (February 1983), pp. 148–53.

Lochman, John J., "Self and Peer Perceptions in Attributional Biases of Aggressive and Non-Aggressive Boys." *Journal of Consulting and Clinical Psychology*, 1987. vol. 55, no. 3, pp. 404–410.

Loss, D., and Ross, J., "Risk Assessment/Interviewing Protocol for Adolescent Sex Offenders." 1987: Mystic, CT

Mahler, Margaret, *Psychological Birth of the Human Infant*, New York: Basic Books, 1975.

Malmquist, C.P., "Children Who Witness Parental Murder: Post Traumatic Aspects," *Journal of American Academy of Child Psychiatry*, vol. XXV (May 1986), pp. 320–26.

Myers, Beverly A., "Psychiatric Problems in Adolescents with Developmental Disabilities" *Journal of American Academy of Child Psychiatry*, vol. XXVI (January 1987), pp. 74–79.

Patterson, Gerald R., *Living With Children*. Champaign, Ill.: Research Press, 1976.

Patterson, Gerald R., *Social Learning Approach to Family Intervention: Coercive Family Process*, vol. 3. Eugene, Ore.: Castalia Publishing Co., 1982.

Pfeffer, C.R., et al, "Predictions of Assaultiveness in Latency Age Children," *American Journal of Psychiatry*, vol. CXL (February 1985), pp. 154–57.

———, et al, "Suicidal Behavior and Assaultive Behavior in Children: Classification, Measurement and Interpretations," *American Journal of Psychiatry*, vol. CXL (February 1985), pp. 154–57.

———, *The Suicidal Child*. New York: The Guilford Press, 1986.

———, "Variables that Predict Assaultiveness in Child Psychiatric Inpatients," *Journal of American Academy of Child Psychiatry*, vol. XXVI (June 1985), pp. 775–80.

Pliszka, Steven R., "Tricyclic Antidepressants in the Treatment of Children with Attention Deficit Disorder," *Jour-*

nal of American Academy of Child Psychiatry, vol. XXVI (February 1987), pp. 127–32.

Pynoos, R.S., "Witness to Violence, the Child Interview," *Journal of American Academy of Child Psychiatry*, vol. XXV (May 1986), pp. 306–20.

Quinton, D., and Rutter, M., "Institutional Rearing, Parenting Difficulties and Marital Support," *Psychological Medicine*, vol. XIV (1984), pp. 107–24.

Redl, Fritz, *The Aggressive Child*. New York: The Free Press, 1957.

Reeves, Jan C.; Werry, John S.; Elkind, Gail S., and Zametkin, M.D., "Attention Deficit, Conduct, Oppositional, and Anxiety Disorders in Children: II. Clinical Characteristics," *Journal of American Academy of Child Psychiatry*, vol. XXVI (February 1987), pp. 144–55.

Robins, L.N., and Rutter, M., *Straight and Devious Pathways from Childhood to Adulthood*. New York: Cambridge University Press, 1990.

Rutter, Michael, et al., *Education, Health and Behavior*. Melbourne, Fla.: Robert E. Krieger Publishing Co., 1970.

———, "Myerian Psychobiology, Personality Development and the Role of Life Experience," *American Journal of Psychiatry*, vol. CXIII (September 1986), pp. 1077–88.

———, et al, *Education, Health and Behavior*. Melbourne, Fla.: Robert E. Krieger Publishing Co., 1970.

———, and Rutter, Giller, *Delinquency*. New York: The Guilford Press, 1983.

———, and Hersov, L., *Child and Adolescent Psychiatry: Modern Approaches*, 2nd ed. St. Louis: C.V. Mosby, 1985.

Sandman, C.A., "The Opiate Hypothesis in Autism and Self-Injury," *Journal of Child and Adolescent Psychopharmacology*, vol. 3, (1991), pp. 237–248.

Satterfield, James H.; Satterfield, Breena, T., and Schell, Anne M., "Therapeutic Interventions to Prevent Delinquency in Hyperactive Boys," *Journal of American Academy of Child Psychiatry*, vol. XXVI (January 1987), pp. 56–64.

Schachar, Russell, "Childhood Hyperactivity," *Journal of Child Psychology and Psychiatry*, vol. 32, no. 1, (1991), pp. 155–191.

Schetky, D.H., "Parental Kidnapping," *Journal of American Academy of Child Psychiatry*, vol. XXIII (May 1983), pp. 279–86.

Sims, Jennifer and Galvin, Matthew, Pediatric Psychopharmacologic Uses of Propranolols, JCPN vol. 3, no. 1 (1990), pp. 18–24.

Spitz, Rene, "Hospitalization," *Psychoanalytic Study of Child*, I, 1945, 53–74 and II, 1946, 113–117.

Stewart, J.T.; Myers, W.C., Burket, R.C., and Lyles, W.B., "A Review of the Pharmacotherapy of Aggression in Children and Adolescents," *Journal of American Academy of Child and Adolescent Psychiatry*, vol. 24, no. 2 (1990) pp. 269–277.

Terr, L.C., "Chowchilla Revisited: The Effects of Psychic Trauma Four Years After a School Bus Kidnapping," *American Journal of Psychiatry*, vol. CXL (December 1983), pp. 1543–51.

Trieschman, Albert E., et al. *The Other Twenty-Three Hours: Childcare Work with Emotionally Disturbed Children in a Therapeutic Milieu.* Hawthorne, N.Y.: Aldine de Gruyter, 1969.

Troy, Michael, and Sroufe, L. Alan, "Victimization Among Preschoolers: Role of Attachment Relationship History," *Journal of American Academy of Child and Adolescent Psychiatry*, vol. XXVI (February 1987), pp. 166–72.

Wallerstein, Judith S., "The Long-term Effect of Divorce on Children: A Review," *Journal of American Academy of Child Psychiatry*, vol. XXX (March 1991), pp. 349–60.

Weiss, Gabrielle and Hechtman, Lily T., *Hyperactive Children Grown Up.* New York: The Guilford Press, 1986.

Werry, John S.; Reeves, Jan Catherina, and Elkind, Gail S., "Attention Deficit, Conduct, Oppositional and Anxiety Disorders in Children: I. A Review of Research on Differentiating Characteristics," *Journal of American Academy of Child Psychiatry*, vol. XXVI (February 1987), pp. 133–43.

Whittaker, James, *Children Away From Home*. Hawthorne, N.Y.: Aldine de Gruyter, 1972.

Winnicott, D.W., *The Family and Individual Development*. New York: Tavistock/Routledge, Chapman and Hall, 1968.

Zametkin, A.S., et al., "Cerebral Glucose Metabolism in Adults Under Hyperactivity of Childhood Onset," *New England Journal of Medicine*, vol. 323, no. 20 (1990) pp. 1361–1367.

Zimet, Sara G., and Farley, Gordon K., "How Do Emotionally Disturbed Children Report Their Competencies and Self-Worth?" *Journal of American Academy of Child and Adolescent Psychiatry*, vol. XXVI (January 1987), pp. 33–38.

INDEX